Building Reading Comprehension

Grades 3-4

by

Jillayne Prince Wallaker

Published by Instructional Fair
an imprint of
Frank Schaffer Publications®

Instructional Fair

Author: Jillayne Prince Wallaker
Editors: Elizabeth Fikkema, Kathryn Wheeler, Judy Tremore
Cover Artist: Matthew Van Zomeren
Interior Artist: Elizabeth Adams

Frank Schaffer Publications®

Instructional Fair is an imprint of Frank Schaffer Publications.

Send all inquiries to:
Frank Schaffer Publications
8720 Orion Place
Columbus, Ohio 43240-2111

Building Reading Comprehension—grades 3–4

ISBN: 1-56822-913-5

12 13 14 PAT 12 11 10 09

Table of Contents

Name _____

When and Where

☞ A setting tells when and where a story takes place. Read the story settings below. Describe where and when the story takes place.

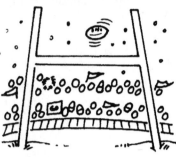

1. The crowd was in an uproar. The West Bend football team had just made a field goal to tie the championship game. Both teams quickly ran off the field to get advice from their coaches. The November snow drifted down, dusting the noisy stadium with white.

   When did the story take place? _____
   Where did the story take place? _____

2. The stars were bright and clear. Ian and his family were gazing at the sky from the hot tub. They watched as several meteors fell. Each one made a bright trail of light across the sky.

   When did the story take place? _____
   Where did the story take place?_____

3. On a sunny, bright July afternoon in 1776, many people were gathering on the commons in Boston. They were getting ready for the big feast planned for the evening.

   When did the story take place? _____
   Where did the story take place?_____

4. The spaceship had been traveling through space for 200 years. The people on board were just coming out of stasis. They hadn't been awake since 2020. The computer was set to wake them up when the planet X59 was a week's travel away.

   When did the story take place? _____
   Where did the story take place?_____

Name _____

Now or Later

☞ Read each setting. Decide whether it happens in the past, the present, or the future. Circle your choice. Highlight the key word or words that helped you decide.

1. In 1492, it was widely believed that monsters lived in the oceans. Travelers worried that their ship would be eaten or sunk before they got where they wanted to go.

    past   present   future

2. Jamie is working on an art project. The background is colored with crayon and he is putting a wash of paint over the top.

    past   present   future

3. It is hot! It is so hot that the ice in Tammi's glass melts before she can drink it. The swing is hanging limply with no one in it. Butch, the dog, is sprawled in the shade with his tongue hanging out. Tammi moves the sprinkler into the shade and turns it on.

    past   present   future

4. Tia and Loe are on their way to grandmother's house. The trip from Jupiter to Earth takes two hours. They haven't been to Earth in a month and they look forward to swimming in the ocean.

    past   present   future

5. The 74-foot-long Brachiosaurus stretched its neck to reach the leaves at the top of the tree. It ripped off a mouthful and munched slowly.

    past   present   future

6. 50-year-old Annie told her granddaughter about third grade, "Back around the year 2000, we were just beginning to use computers in all of the classrooms."

    past   present   future

What's the Problem?

☞ Read each paragraph. Name the characters and state the problem for each.

1. Tanner and Nick were roller skating down the side-walk. Nick hit a stone and fell. His knees and hands slammed into the ground. It was a good thing he was wearing kneepads. His hands were another story.

   Characters: _____

   Problem: _____

2. Bonnie Butterfly flew through the air. She could see for miles. Bonnie was exhausted and hungry and she wanted to land. She felt very comfortable flying, but landing was still hard for her. She caught sight of a patch of delicious-looking flowers. "Oh dear," she thought. "Do I dare land there?"

   Character: _____

   Problem: _____

3. Only three problems out of his thirty-two were done. For the past half-hour Dan had been looking at the page and daydreaming. "Hey, pass your paper up," said Joe. "Mrs. Willis just asked for our work."

   Characters: _____

   Problem: _____

4. Pitter and Patter were drops of water. They had gone many places together during their travels through the water cycle. They traveled through clouds, snowstorms, rivers, and many other places. For the first time, Pitter was going off on her own. She was afraid.

   Characters: _____

   Problem: _____

The Trip

☞ This is the beginning of a story. Read it and use the information to fill in the blanks below.

It was finally getting cooler. After a blazing, hot day, the sun had finally gone down. Abby still couldn't believe their car had broken down. She also couldn't believe her father had decided to walk three miles through the desert for help. The map said there was a town up ahead, but they hadn't seen any cars go by for over an hour.

Abby and her sister Hannah had helped their mother put up the tent and awning so they would have some shade while they waited for their father. So far they had seen some cactus, a couple of

lizards, a nasty, crawling insect, and at least a hundred million grains of hot sand. What a way to begin their spring vacation!

When did the story take place? _____

Where did the story take place? _____

Characters:

_____

Problem:

_____

How do you predict the problem will be solved?

_____

_____

_____

Decision

☞ This is the beginning of a story. Read it and use the information to fill in the blanks below.

The birds are chirping. Little green leaves are just beginning to form on the branches of the trees. Crocuses and early spring flowers bring color to the downtown yards. A gentle breeze whispers of warm weather. Heath is walking slowly with his head down. He does not notice any of the morning's beauty. He has to decide what to do.

Heath's best friend, Shane, wants them to skip school today. Shane has big plans for the day. Shane wants to do daring things. Heath really likes Shane. They are great friends. Heath doesn't want to hurt Shane's feelings or for Shane to think he is a chicken. Still, Heath knows it is wrong to skip school. Heath knows he can get into a world of trouble—at home and at school. And trouble at home would make the school trouble look like a party. Heath suddenly knows what his decision has to be.

When does the story take place? _____

Where does the story take place? _____

Characters:

_____

Problem:

_____

How do you predict the problem will be solved?
Highlight in yellow the details that helped you decide this.

_____

_____

Name _____

Water's Edge

☞ This is the beginning of a story. Read it and use the information to fill in the blanks below.

Gabe walked down to the water. The sun was setting. The sky was blazing with oranges, yellows, pinks, and reds. The tide was coming in. At the edge of the water was an odd-looking creature about one-foot long. Its body seemed to be in three parts. The first part was about three-fourths of a hemisphere. Fitting into the hemisphere was a smaller body part with jagged edges. A long, hard, pointed tail poked its way out of the smaller body part. "What is that thing?" wondered Gabe. "Can it hurt me?"

He saw Hannah walking towards him on the beach and called her over. "Do you know what this is?" he asked.

"It's a horseshoe crab," replied Hannah. "My older sister studies them. She knows a lot about horseshoe crabs."

"Great," said Gabe. "I want to know more about them."

When does the story take place? _____

Where does the story take place? _____

Characters:

_____

Problem:

_____

How do you predict the problem will be solved?
Highlight in yellow the details that helped you decide this.

_____

_____

_____

Power's Out

When a severe storm comes, you may lose electrical power. There are things you can do to prepare for a power outage.

First of all, you need a non-electrical light source, such as a flashlight, lantern, or candles. Make sure you have fresh batteries, fuel for the lantern, or matches for the candles. A battery-powered radio will help you get weather and emergency information. It is a good idea to unplug equipment, such as answering machines, computers, televisions, and microwaves. Lightning strikes or power surges can damage these items.

If a storm is coming that may cause the power to be out for more than just a few hours, you will want to prepare some other items. Fill empty milk jugs with fresh water if you have an electric well for water. Use the jugs of water for drinking, cooking over a camp stove, and flushing toilets. Keep healthy foods on hand that can be prepared and eaten without the use of electricity, such as fruit, bread, and peanut butter. If you live in an area with cold weather, you will need a plan to keep warm. Even if you have gas heat, most furnaces have electric starters. Find extra blankets or purchase a generator with gasoline to run the furnace.

Being prepared for a power outage can make the difference between a serious problem and a cozy family experience.

☞ Use the information above to write in the solution to each problem. Highlight where you found the information in the text.

Problem	Solution
The television is out and you cannot listen to the news for information about the storm.	
The well has stopped working so you cannot flush the toilet.	
The furnace won't start and it is getting very cold in the house.	
You are hungry and your electric stove doesn't work.	
The power is out and it is dark in the house.	

Highlighting Information

☞ Highlighting is a strategy that will help you remember what you read. While you read, look for words or phrases that will help you remember details. Follow the five directions to highlight words in the sentences below.

1. Highlight three tools you can use for highlighting.

   When you highlight, use a light-colored crayon, pencil, or marker to color over the word or phrase.

2. Find the three key action words in the next sentence and highlight with yellow.

   When you are reading a passage, read the paragraph carefully; then scan the paragraph for key words; and finally, highlight those words.

3. What should you highlight? Highlight the two words.

   When highlighting, look for a word or phrase that will help you remember the thought.

4. Two phrases tell you what to do if your marker is a dark color. Highlight each phrase with a dark color. Do not include the word "or."

   If you use a darker color, you can choose to either mark over the words lightly or underline the words.

5. You may use highlighting in many reading materials. Highlight the materials.

   Highlighting is a good strategy when you are reading from copied pages, testing materials, newspapers, or your own books. Never highlight in a school or library book or a book that someone else may use.

Which Resource?

Information can be found in many places. Knowing where to look for information can make locating it much faster.

One place to look for factual information is in an encyclopedia. An encyclopedia usually has many volumes. Each volume lists topics in alphabetical order.

Another source for information is an atlas. An atlas is full of maps. If you're looking for words instead of places, a thesaurus is a great tool for finding words that mean about the same thing. A dictionary is a good book to look in for spelling, meanings, and pronunciations, or for learning how to say a word.

An index or glossary may be found in the back of some books. An index lists topics in alphabetical order and gives the page numbers where you can find that information. A glossary is like a dictionary of words used within that book.

atlas   dictionary   encyclopedia   glossary   thesaurus   index

☞ Write the best resource on the line.

1. _____ Find the page in the book that tells about limpets.

2. _____ Locate a map of South America.

3. _____ A word in the textbook is in bold print. What is its definition?

4. _____ How do you say "pyrargyrite"?

5. _____ Find five words that mean the same thing as "happy."

6. _____ What are the names and spellings of the world's oceans?

7. _____ Find five facts about kites.

8. _____ You are looking for a word that is more polite than "vomited" for your newspaper article.

9. _____ You are working on equivalent fractions and want to know which pages in your math book cover this topic.

Name _____

Rainsticks

A rainstick is a musical instrument. It has been used since ancient times. A rainstick looks like a branch from a tree that has been cut off. Although it looks heavy, it is not. It is very light. When you tip it, you hear a calm, quiet noise like rainfall.

The rainstick is not made from wood. It is made from the skeleton of a cactus. In Chili, rainsticks are made from dead quisco or copado cactus plants. When the cactus dies, the skin and thorns fall off, leaving the normata, or skeleton. The inside of the normata is hollow. Thorns are pounded into the inside. The thorns are pounded in a spiral formation. Tiny stones are put inside before the ends are sealed.

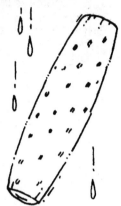

The tiny stones pour across the thorns when the rainstick is tilted. This makes the soothing sound of rain that gives the musical instrument its name.

1. What is a normata? _____

   Highlight where you found the answer with red.

2. What is a copado? _____

   Highlight where you found the answer with yellow.

3. What causes the rainstick to make a noise like rain? _____

   _____

   Highlight details that helped you decide this with green.

4. Name three things used to make the rainstick. _____

   _____

5. Find two words that describe the sound a rainstick makes. Then think of another word that means about the same thing that you can add to your list.

   _____

Wolf Talk

Wolves are the wild relatives of our family dogs. Wolves live in family groups. Most groups, or packs, have from six to ten members. Scientists have found that wolves communicate, or talk, to one another. The wolves use their voices and their bodies to tell each other important information.

Wolves are best known for their howling. They howl to tell other wolves to stay away. They may also howl to call each other back to the pack. A wolf may snarl or growl if danger is near or another wolf is threatening. Wolves may bark a warning or a challenge.

When one wolf wants to tell another it is the boss, it will keep its head high and ears forward. Its tail will also be held high, but not wagging. It will stare directly at the wolf with which it is communicating and keep its mouth relaxed.

When a wolf's head is down and its ears are back, it is saying it doesn't want any trouble. This wolf will keep its mouth closed and its eyes turned away from the other wolf. It may also tuck its tail between its legs and possibly roll on its back and show its belly. This lets another wolf know it definitely does not want to get into a fight.

When a wolf wants to play, it looks much like a playful house dog. This wolf will go down on its front paws with its tail in the air like it is bowing. The tail will wag. Its ears will be forward and its mouth will be smiling with the tongue hanging out.

The next time you watch a dog, think about its wolf relative. Maybe the dog is trying to tell you something.

☞ What is each wolf below communicating?

1. Its tail is high, but not wagging.

    _____

    _____

2. The wolf is down on its front paws with its tail in
    the air. _____

    _____

3. It has a relaxed mouth and direct look.

    _____

    _____

4. The wolf rolls on its back and shows its belly.

    _____

    _____

5. The wolf's tail is between its legs.

    _____

    _____

6. The mouth is smiling and ears are forward.

    _____

    _____

Write one fact about wolf life. Highlight where you found the fact in the story.

_____

_____

_____

Red Tide

The Gulf of Mexico is a body of saltwater that lies between Florida and Central America. It is a place where many people like to go on vacation. The weather is almost always warm. People like to go swimming and play in the sun. And many interesting plants and animals live in the water, such as dolphins, sharks, horseshoe crabs, and sponges. But once in a while the "red tide" comes and spoils the fun.

When the red tide comes, the water turns red. The water may stay red for a couple hours or several months. When the water is red, everyone stays out because the red tide can make people sick. Red tide is caused by a tiny organism called a dinoflagellate (di nuh FLAJ uh late) that multiplies when the nutrients, sunlight, and water are just right.

People do not like the red tide because they know that it might irritate their eyes, nose, and throats. Some people find that their lips and tongues tingle. People with asthma may find it hard to breathe.

The red tide can be poison to fish and other marine, or saltwater, animals. When the sea animals eat the organism, they are poisoned and die. Other animals die because the organism use up all the oxygen in the water and the

sea animals cannot breathe. Many fish wash up on shore during a red tide. The dead fish smell terrible.

Some shellfish eat the red tide and do not die. But the poisons can stay in the bodies of shellfish. When there is a red tide, it is unsafe for people and other animals to eat foods like oysters and clams.

Most people do not spend as much time on the beach during red tide. This is because of the health risks and the smell of rotting marine bodies. However, people who like to look for shells find that red tide is a good time to collect them. The poisons kill the animals inside the seashells and the shells wash up on the beaches.

Some scientists in western Florida are studying the red tides. They hope to be able to learn more about them. Learning more will help scientists understand why they happen. Then they will be able to warn the coastal people when the water is not safe.

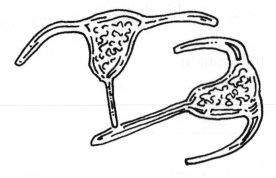

☞ Read the article on the Red Tide and complete the following.

1. Why are scientists studying the red tides? _____

_____

2. What does *marine* mean in this article? _____

3. Name two conditions that seem to cause the red tide to multiply. _____

_____

_____

4. Name three ways a red tide can affect people.

_____

_____

_____

5. In this article, what does *multiply* mean? _____

_____

6. What organism causes the red tide? _____

7. What are some nice features about the Gulf of Mexico? _____

_____

_____

8. What people like to stay at the beach during red tide? _____

_____

9. What should a person with asthma do when there is a red tide?

_____

A Beautiful Butterfly

Most people can easily recognize the monarch butterfly. It has distinctive orange, black, and white markings. This beautiful butterfly is only one part of the monarch life cycle.

The monarch butterfly lays pin-head-sized eggs on milkweed plants. Soon these eggs hatch. A very hungry caterpillar comes out. This yellow, black, and white caterpillar eats milkweed plants for about ten days before it hangs upside down in a "J" shape, then transforms into a chrysalis.

While in the tissue-paper-thin chrysalis, the sixteen-legged caterpillar changes into a six-legged butterfly. After a week, a wet, crumpled butterfly emerges from the chrysalis. It slowly pumps fluids from its abdomen into the crumpled wings.

Just 15 minutes after the butterfly emerges, its wings are extended, dry, and ready for flight.

Monarchs have powerful wings, which allow them to migrate long distances. When the weather gets cold in the fall, they may migrate as far as from Michigan to South America.

In the spring, the monarchs make the long trip back north where they lay their eggs on milkweed plants. The cycle begins again.

☞ Draw a sketch of the monarch life cycle here.

☞ Read the article and complete the following.

1. Reread the first paragraph. Find the two words that tell the topic of this article.

    _____   _____

2. The author wants to tell . . .   about the monarch life cycle.

                                        what the monarch looks like.

                                        that monarch butterflies migrate.

3. What are the four stages of the monarch life cycle?

    _____ _____ _____ _____

4. What are the three colors of the caterpillar? _____

    _____

5. How many legs does the caterpillar have? _____

6. For how many days is the monarch a caterpillar? _____

7. What does the caterpillar eat? _____

8. In what shape does the monarch caterpillar hang before becoming a chrysalis?

    _____

9. How long is the monarch inside the chrysalis? _____

10. About how long does it take for the monarch's wings to dry? _____

11. What are the three colors of the monarch butterfly?_____

    _____

12. How many legs does the butterfly have? _____

13. What do monarch butterflies do in the fall? _____

14. What do they do in the spring? _____

Math Homework

Dear Meg,

    I am sorry that you are sick. I have your class work for you. We learned how to subtract with regrouping today. Here are the directions.

1. Look at the problem.
2. Put your finger on the ones column.
3. Decide whether you can subtract the bottom ones digit from the top ones digit.
4. If yes, go to number 9. If no, go to number 5.
5. Pretend you are picking up a cup of ten. Cross out the top tens digit.
6. If you take one ten, how many tens do you have left? Write the number above the ten you crossed out.
7. Add the cup of ten to the ones. Look at how many ones you have.
8. Cross out the top ones digit. Write the number above the one you crossed out.
9. Subtract the ones.
10. Subtract the tens.

Good luck! I hope this helps you. If you have questions, please call me tonight.

Kristine

☞ Refer to the letter to complete the following. Highlight where you found answers.

1. In which column should Meg start subtracting? _____

2. What is Meg's next step if she can subtract the bottom ones digit from the top ones digit? _____

3. What is Meg's next step if she cannot subtract the bottom ones digit from the top ones digit? _____

4. Look at these problems. Decide whether Meg can subtract the ones column. Write *yes* under these problems. Write *no* under problems that must go to step 5.

$$\begin{array}{cccc}
74 & 90 & 58 & 35 \\
-37 & -71 & -45 & -16 \\
\hline
\end{array}$$

Name _____

Pizza Recipe

☞ To make delicious pizzas, follow these directions.

Ingredients:
soft tortillas
tomato sauce
shredded mozzarella cheese
your favorite pizza toppings: pepperoni, mushrooms, pineapple, sausage, olives, etc.

1. Gather the ingredients, a cookie sheet, and a spoon.
2   Put the tortillas on the cookie sheet.
3. Spoon tomato sauce onto each tortilla. Spread it around to lightly cover the tortilla.
4. Sprinkle with mozzarella cheese.
5. Add other toppings that you like.
6. Bake at 350° for about 10 minutes or until cheese is melted.
7. Take out of oven and let cool for 3 to 5 minutes.
8. Remove from pan and serve.

☞ Refer to the recipe to complete the following. Highlight where you found answers.

1. List three possible toppings for your pizza.

    _____   _____   _____

2. If you like ground beef, could you use it as a topping? _____

    What words tell you this? _____

3. Can hard-shelled tacos be used with this recipe?   Yes   No

4. At what temperature should you bake your pizza? _____ For how long? _____

5. What ingredient goes on the tortilla first? _____

6. Which goes on first—the toppings or cheese? _____

7. If you could choose any three toppings to go on your pizza, what would they be?

    _____   _____   _____

    Circle: I found this answer in . . . a) the text.   b) my head.   c) a book.

Note Home

☞ Ms. Trasker sends the third-grade schedule home so the parents and students know what to expect for the following week.

Dear Parents and Students,

Here are the highlights for next week:

Monday: art, assembly

Tuesday: library check-out, math homework night

Wednesday: music, lunch money due

Thursday: technology, social studies test

Friday: gym, book orders due

This is what we will be studying:

Reading:

We will be locating story elements: setting, characters, problem, and solution.

Mathematics:

We will practice regrouping three-digit numbers with adding and subtracting.

Science:

We are learning to identify minerals through field tests.

Social Studies:

The maps and globes unit is coming to a close. The test is on Thursday. Be sure to look over the attached study sheet and study questions.

Upcoming field trip:

We will be going to the quarry and the Rock and Mineral Museum a week from Wednesday. Be sure to send in $1.50. If any parents are able to join us, please send a note by Friday. No siblings, please.

Name _____

☞ Refer to the note home to complete the following information.

1. List the story elements on which the class is working. _____

_____

2. What day does the class have music? _____

3. If a parent can come on the field trip, what should he or she do?

_____

4. What is attached to this note? _____

_____

5. How is the class learning to identify minerals? _____

_____

6. What kind of numbers is the class using to regroup?

_____

7. What day is the social studies test? _____

8. How much does the field trip cost? _____

9. What day should students bring their library books? _____

10. Pretend this is your schedule for the week. Write yourself one reminder for each
    day of the week.

Monday	Tuesday	Wednesday	Thursday	Friday

Book Offer

GET SIX GREAT BOOKS FOR UNDER A BUCK!

99¢   99¢

Choose your favorite six books from our huge catalog of great titles.

Write the four-digit code for each book in the spaces on the form below. You will be billed 99¢ for each book, plus tax and postage and handling.

Here is the deal: *Buy six titles today at this incredible price, then you only have to purchase six additional books at regular club prices. You have one year to make your purchases.

Enter your selection numbers here:

_ _ _ _, _ _ _ _, _ _ _ _

_ _ _ _, _ _ _ _, _ _ _ _

SPECIAL OFFER!

Order a seventh book today at only $3.99 and you only have 5 more to go!

_ _ _ _

Offer expires 11/30/04

Name _____

Address _____

City, State, Zip_____

_____ bill me _____ payment enclosed

Credit card number: _____

*We reserve the right to substitute titles if the one ordered is out of stock.

Name _____

☞ Refer to the advertisement to complete this page.

1. What product is this advertisement trying to sell you?

    movies   tapes   books   stocks

2. What is the greatest number of books you can purchase with this form? _____

3. After you buy the first six books, how many books do you need to buy? _____

4. How long do you have to buy them? _____

5. 99¢ is the price for . . .   all six books.   each of the six books.

6. Decide whether each statement is true or false. Write *T* for true and *F* for false. Then, go back to the advertisement and highlight where you found the answer.

    _____ You are guaranteed the titles you select.

    _____ You can order one more book for $3.99.

    _____ The offer is good though December.

    _____ You can send the payment or have the company bill you.

☞ Write *given* or *not given* to describe whether the advertisement gave you this information. Highlight where you found the answer.

7. How much is postage and handling? _____

8. What is the average price of a book at "regular club prices"? _____

9. What is the telephone number to call for more information? _____

10. Write two or three sentences telling what you think about this offer. Do you think it is a good deal? Explain your answer. _____

    _____

    _____

    _____

Cancel It

☞ Jane wrote the following letter to Video Store. Read the letter and complete the following.

July 23, 2003

Jane Price
16 Tan Street
Troy, MI 49000

Video Store
Customer Service
14 E. Park Road
Richmond, VA 23001

To Whom It May Concern:

Please find enclosed the $8.22 payment for the video "Learning with Bally." We look forward to receiving our free cassette tape, "Bally in Concert." My brother and I love the video and look forward to listening to the cassette while traveling in our car.

We would also like to cancel our membership immediately. Our membership number is #549RN9J96. Thank you for your prompt handling of this request.

Sincerely,

Jane Price

#549RN9J96

---

1. Give two reasons Jane wrote this letter.

   _____

   _____

2. Does Jane want to get more videos from this company?

   _____

   _____

   Highlight information that helped you decide this.

3. Where does Jane live?

   _____

   _____

4. Jane wrote #549RN9J96 after her name. What is it?

   _____

   _____

   Highlight the sentence that gave you the information.

5. Is this a friendly letter or a business letter? _____

   _____

   What makes you think so? _____

   _____

Name _____

Understanding Food Labels

Nutrition Facts	Cracker A	Cracker B	Cracker C
Serving Size	5 crackers (30 g)	5 crackers (15 g)	15 crackers (30 g)
Servings Per Container	About 15	About 28	About 15
Calories	70	80	150
Calories from Fat	10	50	60

Food labels provide a lot of information. However, they can be tricky to read. Read parts of three food labels, above.

Look at the serving sizes. Notice that cracker A and cracker B seem to have the same serving size. They both have 5 crackers. However, when you look at how many grams are in each serving, cracker A actually has the same serving size as cracker C, not cracker B.

Analyze the nutritional information on the three labels. Transfer the information to the chart and answer the questions below. When you are comparing, it is important to compare the same amounts. Write the information for 30 grams of cracker B.

	Grams	# of Crackers	Calories
A	30		
B	30		
C	30		

1. Which cracker is larger, cracker A or cracker B?

   _____

   How can you tell? _____

   _____

2. Which one has the most calories for 30 grams?

   _____

3. Which cracker is larger, cracker A or cracker C?

   _____

   How can you tell? _____

   _____

4. Which cracker has the fewest calories per equal-sized serving? _____

Name _____

Flags

☞ Read about the flags from six different countries. On the next page, the six flags are pictured. Identify the flags and complete the information below each flag. Refer to the descriptions to color the flags.

Australia is a country where kangaroos live. In the upper left corner of its flag, there is a cross overlapping a criss-cross. It has one large star and five small stars. The flag has three colors: dark blue, red, and white. The stars are white. The field, or background, is dark blue. The + and x are both red outlined in white. The continent has the same name as this country.

Brazil is the largest country in South America. The Amazon River Basin is in Brazil. The flag from Brazil has a circle within a diamond. The flag has four colors: light blue, green, white, and yellow. The center circle is light blue with a white stripe and white stars. The writing in the white stripe is the same color blue as the circle. The diamond around the circle is yellow. The outer rectangle is green.

China is a country in Asia. Mount Everest is located in China. China's flag is mostly red. In the upper left corner, it contains a large star and four small stars in a semi-circle to the right of the large star. Each star is yellow.

Ghana is a country in Africa that borders the Atlantic Ocean. This country exports cocoa, gold, and timber. Ghana's flag has three horizontal stripes. There is a single star in the center stripe. The flag is made up of four colors: black, green, yellow, and red. The star is black and is in the yellow middle stripe. The top stripe is red and the bottom one is green.

Guatemala is in Central America. This country has 27 volcanoes and often has earthquakes. The flag has three vertical stripes. It has two colors: light blue and white. The outside stripes are light blue. The middle stripe is white. There is a decoration in the middle of the white stripe.

Almost half of the **Netherlands** is below sea level. Dikes hold seawater off the land. The flag from the Netherlands has three horizontal stripes. The top stripe is red. The middle stripe is white. The bottom stripe is blue. The Netherlands are in northern Europe.

☞ following directions

Name ______________________

☞ Read the article. Complete the information about each country and color its flag.

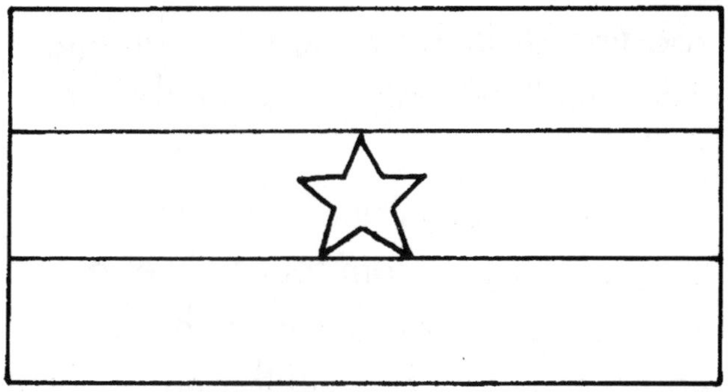

Country: ______________________

Continent: ______________________

Fact: ______________________

Country: ______________________

Continent: ______________________

Fact: ______________________

Country: ______________________

Continent: ______________________

Fact: ______________________

Country: ______________________

Continent: ______________________

Fact: ______________________

Country: ______________________

Continent: ______________________

Fact: ______________________

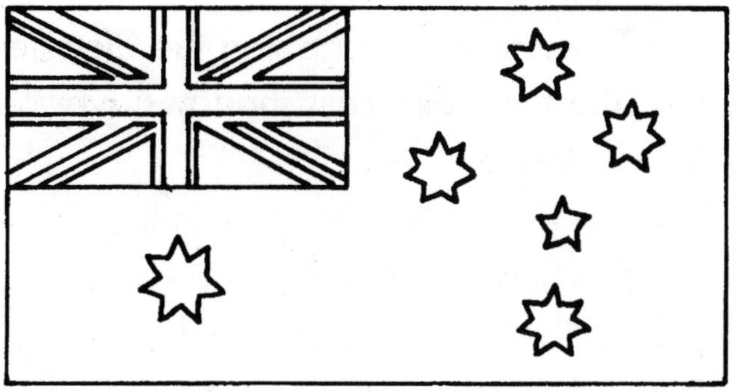

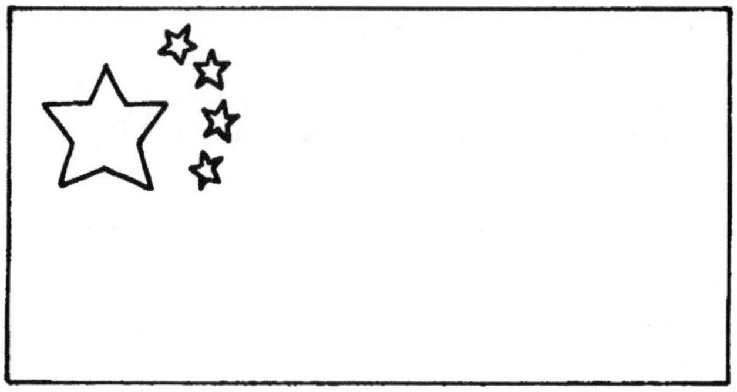

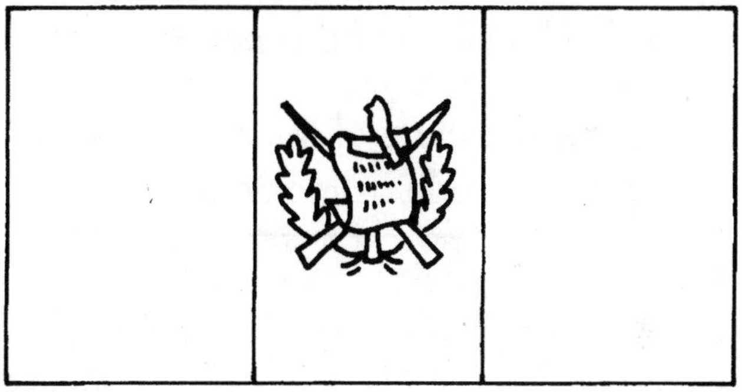

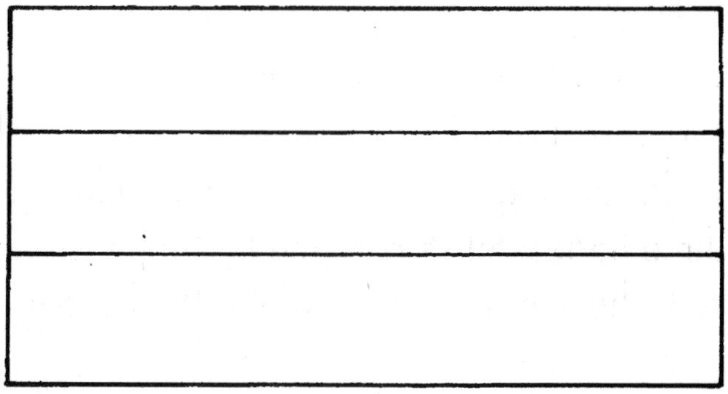

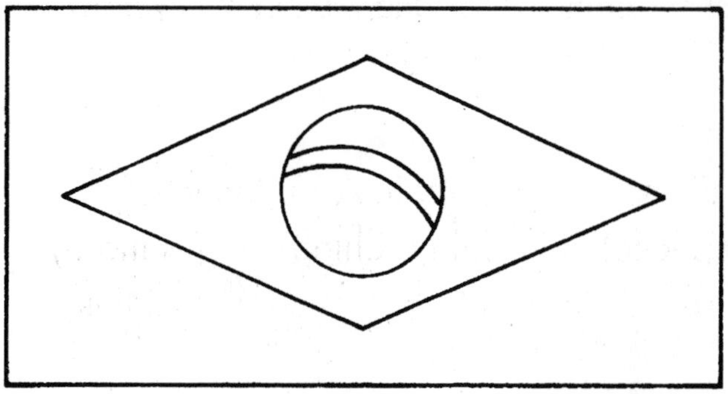

Country: ______________________

Continent: ______________________

Fact: ______________________

Name _____

Marshmallows

The stars were bright in the October sky. The full moon cast shadows over the backyard.

The fire burned brightly in the fire pit. The flames glowed orange, then yellow, then red. The logs cracked and popped. Sparks drifted up, floated off, and went out. At the edge of the fire pit were glowing embers. Their colors shifted from black to orange to white.

It was time for roasting marshmallows. Each child found a perfect roasting stick. They speared white marshmallows onto the ends of their sticks.

The two boys and three girls ranged in ages from four to twelve. Their parents watched from the four chairs scattered around the fire.

As each marshmallow was roasted a golden brown, it went into a mouth. Then new marshmallows were popped onto the ends of the sticks and the roasting began again.

☞ Draw a picture of the story. Each time you draw a detail, highlight it in the story. Include as many details as you can.

Starting Out Right

☞ Each paragraph is missing its topic sentence. Write an X in front of the topic sentence that makes the most sense for each paragraph.

It is wet and cold, but you can do so many things with it. You can make snowballs and throw them at a target. You can make forts, igloos, and snowmen from snow. You need it for sledding down a hill, and no one could make snow angels without it.

1. ____ Snow is lots of fun.

____ Winter is a very cold time of the year.

____ It is fun to throw snowballs.

_____

When he comes to a word he doesn't know, Ian uses many strategies. He rereads the sentence to think about what word would make sense. He looks for familiar chunks in words. He uses expression when he reads and he can explain what he has just read.

2. ____ Rereading is an important skill.

____ Ian is a good reader.

____ Ian reads with expression.

_____

If you did put your tongue on metal, it would stick. Your warm tongue melts the frozen surface of the metal. Then the icy metal refreezes to the wet surface of your tongue. When you try to pull off your tongue, the top layer of skin may remain frozen to the metal. Ouch!

3. ____ Don't put your tongue on ice-cold metal.

____ When the temperature drops, things freeze.

____ Tongues are used to taste.

_____

Without it, it would be difficult to learn. School provides us with the materials to learn and professional people to teach us. We are lucky that we can go to school. Some countries do not allow all children to attend school.

4. ____ It is fun to do math and science.

____ Teachers are important people.

____ School is important.

Name _____

What's The Point?

☞ Each paragraph is missing its topic sentence. Read the rest of the paragraph and decide what it is about. Complete the guide below each paragraph to help you write the topic sentence.

1. _____

It keeps your brain working. It helps you concentrate and not feel tired. Breakfast also gives you the energy to do your best.

Word referent (pronoun): _____ Word it refers to (topic): _____

The point of the paragraph is _____ .

2. _____

It can make writing a story or a paper much easier. You can add an idea in the middle of a sentence without rewriting the whole sentence. The computer can also check the spelling for you.

Word referent (pronoun): _____ Word it refers to (topic): _____

The point of the paragraph is _____ .

3. _____

They eat grass. They also eat other small plants. In the winter, if green plants are hard to find, deer also eat bark from trees.

Word referent (pronoun): _____ Word it refers to (topic): _____

The point of the paragraph is _____ .

Sharp Pencils & Sharp Minds

☞ Read each paragraph. Fill in the blanks

You need a sharp pencil in order to do quality work. What should you do if your pencil tip breaks while someone is giving instructions? It can be distracting to sharpen your pencil during instruction time. It is important to know when to sharpen your pencil so that learning continues for everyone in the class. Some good times to sharpen a pencil are before or after school and at recess. Another possible time is when people are working, not listening to directions. When students are trying to listen to another student, the teacher, or a video presentation, the pencil sharpener can be distracting or loud enough to make hearing difficult. Keep an extra sharp pencil in your desk so you have a pencil at a time when you may not be able to get to the sharpener.

Topic: _____

Main idea of the paragraph:_____

Choose two of the supporting details to write here. _____

_____

_____

Most nine- and ten-year-olds need from 9 to 12 hours of sleep each night. Getting enough rest improves your attitude. It helps your brain stay in the thinking mode rather than falling into the emotional mode. It helps you stay focused on learning and allows you to think clearly. Most rested people get along better with others than their sleepy friends do. They have more energy not only for learning but also for playing.

Topic: _____

Main idea of the paragraph:_____

Choose two of the supporting details to write here. _____

_____

_____

Wolves

☞ Read the paragraph. Underline the topic sentence and write it in the large oval. Find the two main supporting details. Write them in the next set of ovals. Each supporting detail has minor supporting details. Write them in the last set of ovals.

At one time, gray wolves lived all over the United States. After the settlement of the Europeans in the US, the wolf population quickly became endangered. By the 1930s, wolves were gone from most of the west, including Yellowstone National Park. Some wolves were killed because they ate livestock. Others moved to avoid living near people. In the 1990s, wolves returned to the western United States and Yellowstone National Park. Some wolves were brought back to parks and wild regions by rangers and scientists. Some wolves moved from Canada back to the Wyoming park. Scientists and wolf supporters are watching the progress of the wolf populations. They hope the wolf will no longer be classified as an endangered or threatened species.

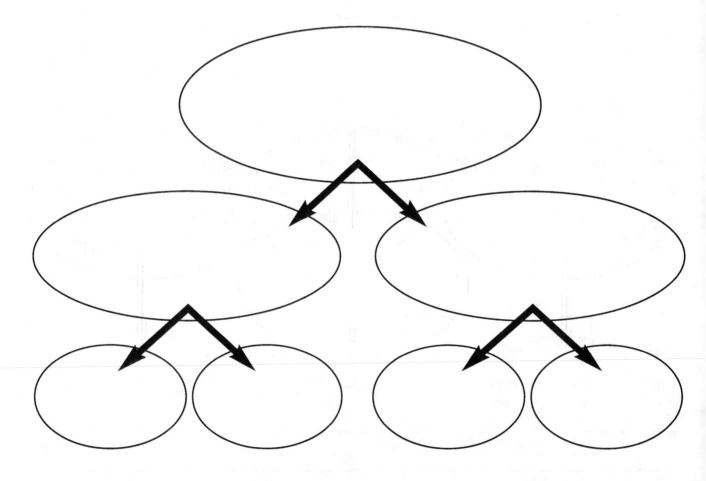

Long Necks

☞ Read the paragraph. Underline the topic sentence and write it in the large oval. Find and write the three main supporting details in the next set of ovals. Each supporting detail has minor supporting details. Write one in each of the last set of ovals.

Paleontologists have found many long-necked dinosaurs that lived in the Jurassic period. One such dinosaur is the Brachiosaurus. This dinosaur was around 70 feet long. Its front legs were longer than its hind legs. It walked on all four legs and its back sloped down from its shoulders. A second long-necked dinosaur was Apatosaurus. This dinosaur has also been called Brontosaurus. Apatosaurus was around 70 feet long. Its front legs were shorter than its hind legs. It walked on all four legs and its back sloped toward its neck. A third long-necked dinosaur was the Diplodocus. It was around 88 feet long. Most of its length was from its long neck and even longer tail. The diplodocus probably used its whiplike tail as a weapon against attackers.

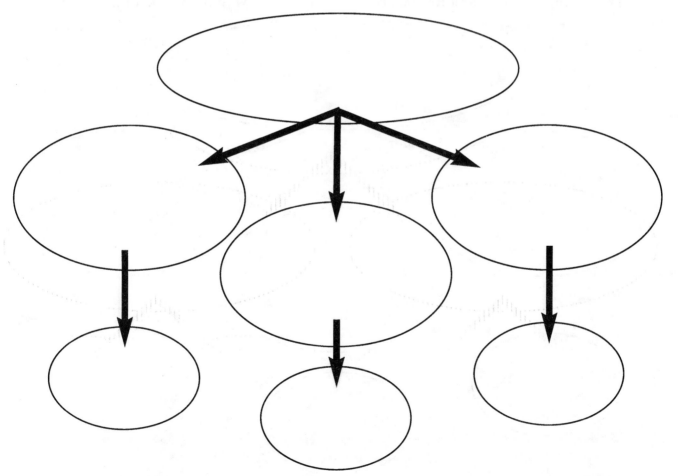

Name _____

Great Lakes

☞ Read the paragraph. Underline the topic sentence and write it in the large oval. Find the three main supporting details. Write them in the next set of ovals. Each supporting detail has minor supporting details. Write one for each in the last set of ovals.

Many states border the five Great Lakes in the United States. One state is Michigan. Michigan touches four of the Great Lakes: Lake Michigan, Lake Superior, Lake Huron, and Lake Erie. The Mackinaw Bridge joins the narrow passage where Lake Michigan and Lake Huron meet. Michigan beaches are full during the summer with swimmers and boaters. Michigan supports many state parks that border the Great Lakes.

Wisconsin is a state that touches two Great Lakes. It is on the west side of Lake Michigan and to the south of Lake Superior. Many people launch boats from this state. People catch freshwater fish in all seasons. Tourists visit and enjoy the water of Wisconsin in different ways.

Illinois borders the southern part of Lake Michigan. Chicago is a large city right on the lake. Navy Pier is one Chicago tourist attraction on the lake. Visitors and people from Illinois enjoy the lake for swimming, boating, and viewing.

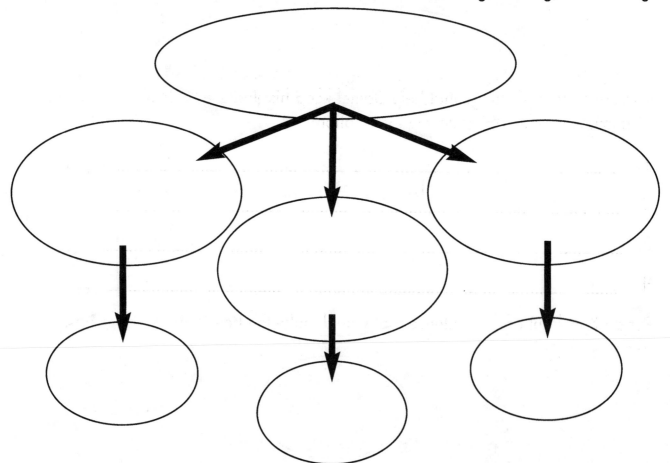

Name _____

Messy Desk

☞ The students in Megan's class were assigned to interview other students about something they were good at. Here is Megan's interview with Daniel.

Megan:	I noticed that you have a clean desk. What do you do to keep your desk clean?
Daniel:	I first decide what has to go into my desk. Then, I find a place for everything and try to keep it in its place.
Megan:	How do you find time to do this?
Daniel:	On Tuesdays, I take a few minutes to make sure my desk is clean.
Megan:	So, you choose a day to work on your desk?
Daniel:	Yes.
Megan:	Then you only clean your desk on Tuesday?
Daniel:	No, whenever I take something out, I try to do it witout making a mess. And when I put something back, I try to put it in its place.
Megan:	Does this really work?
Daniel:	Most of the time. When it gets a little messy, I know it will get straightened out on Tuesday.
Megan:	Thank you for your time, Daniel.

Megan needs to write a summary of her interview with Daniel. Help her plan her summary. List four things that help Daniel keep his desk clean. Highlight key words or phrases where you found the information.

1. _____

2. _____

3. _____

4. _____

Put an X in front of the sentence that would make the best topic sentence for Megan's summary.

____ Tuesday is a good day to clean desks.

____ Keeping your desk clean takes planning and time.

____ A messy desk is bad.

____ Put things back in their place when you are finished with them.

Deep in the Earth

The earth is covered with rocks of various sizes, colors, and shapes. Rocks may be formed in different ways. Three kinds of rocks are igneous rocks, sedimentary rocks, and metamorphic rocks.

Igneous rocks are formed from extremely high temperatures. Deep inside the earth's core is hot, liquid rock called magma. Magma may be forced through cracks in the earth. As it moves away from the hot core, it cools and forms igneous rock. Sometimes liquid rock is forced to the surface of the earth through volcanoes. When lava from a volcano cools, it forms igneous rock.

Sedimentary rock is formed when loose materials are pressed together over time. These loose materials may be small stones, sand, and decomposed plants and animals. Often the materials accumulate on the bottom of the ocean. The water may dissolve or get pressed out. The loose materials get cemented together as they harden into rock.

Metamorphic rocks are rocks that have been formed by some major change. Pressure and heat can change igneous and sedimentary rocks into metamorphic rocks. Through heat and pressure, the metamorphic rock may change the way it looks or even its mineral makeup.

Each of these rocks can be found on the earth's crust. You can study a rock's properties to help identify whether it is igneous, sedimentary, or metamorphic.

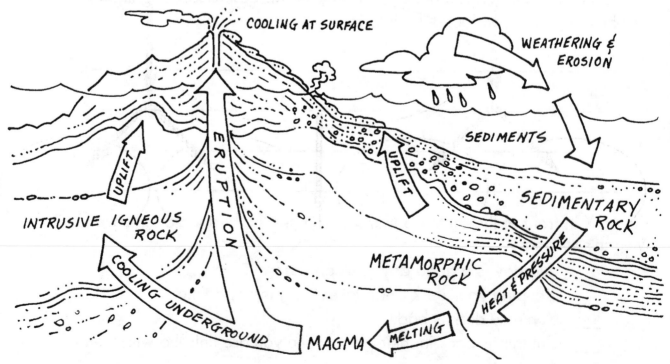

☞ Refer to the article to complete the following.

1. Use one word to name the topic of this passage. _____

2. The main idea of the passage is . . .   Fossils are trapped in rocks.

                                       Igneous rocks are formed from magma.

                                       Rocks are formed three ways.

3. Fill in the web. Write the topic sentence in the first oval. Write the three sub-topics in the next three ovals. Fill in the rest of the ovals with the supporting details.

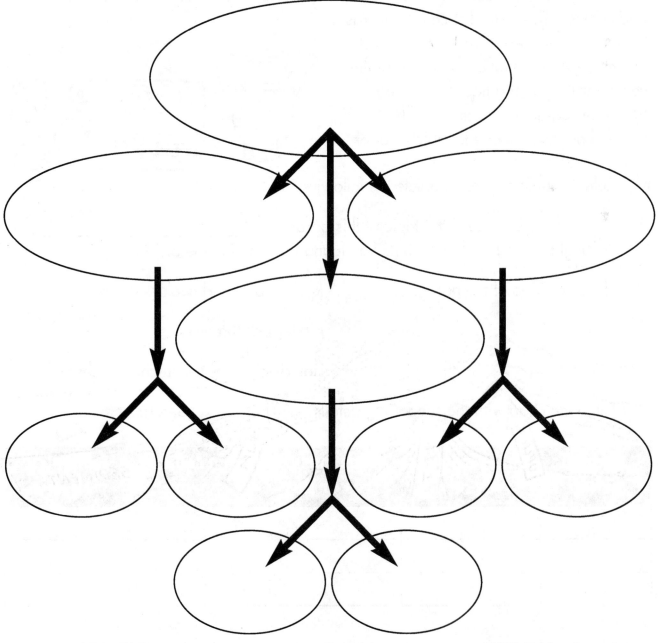

Solids, Liquids, and Gases

Everything is made up of matter. Matter may appear in three different forms, or states: solids, liquids, or gases. The first state is solid. All solids take up space and have mass. They also have a definite shape. If you place a solid object in a container, the object stays the same shape. Examples of solids are rocks, cork, and cookies. The second state of matter is liquid. A liquid also takes up space and has mass. A liquid takes the shape of the container it is in. If a liquid is poured from one container into another, the liquid changes its shape to match that of its new container. Examples of liquids are water, milk, and pop. The third state of matter is gas. Gases take up space and have mass. Like liquids, they take the shape of the container they are in. Examples of gases are oxygen, hydrogen, and carbon dioxide. Solids, liquids, and gases are the three states of matter.

☞ Refer to the article to complete the following.

1. Use one word to name the topic of this paragraph. _____
    Highlight in the text the first time you found this word in the article.

2. The main idea of the paragraph is . . .   Rocks, cork, and cookies are solids.

    Matter has three states.

    Liquids and gases can change shape.

3. Fill in the chart with the supporting details.

State of matter	Takes up space (yes or no)	Has mass (yes or no)	Changes shape (yes or no)	Examples (list)

A Night in Texas

Dear Hailey,

We are in Austin, Texas. You would never believe what I saw tonight. We were in a restaurant by the Congress Avenue Bridge. As the sun was going down, I saw a cloud moving around by the bridge. Do you know what the cloud was? It was bats!! The bats live under the bridge. It is dark there during the day because the sun does not shine under the bridge. Also, the sun makes it nice and warm, kind of like my electric blanket at home.

Well, when the sun started to go down, all of those bats woke up. They were hungry. The waitress said there were over a million of the Mexican free-tailed bats that live under the Congress Avenue Bridge. I wanted to know if they attacked the cars or the people walking on the bridge. She laughed and said that bats are gentle animals that may look scary, but they do not attack people or cars.

Another waitress said the bats were really good because they eat over 10,000 pounds of insects EVERY NIGHT! Gag, can you imagine eating that many bugs? I weigh about 60 pounds so that's like eating enough insects to make about 170 of me. Boy, maybe we need some of those bats by our house. I sure hated all of those mosquitoes that were trying to eat us last week.

Well, I've got to go. Don't get too "batty" without me!
                    Sincerely,
                    Mikaela

1. Where was Mikaela when she wrote the letter? _____

2. What is the topic of her letter? (one word) _____

3. Write three details Mikaela wrote about her topic. _____

_____

_____

4. Mikaela compared several things to other things. Write one comparison here.

_____ to _____

5. Write one fact you learned about bats. _____

_____

Name _____

Walk by Water

Jade is walking along the edge of the water. She shivers a little and buttons her sweater. The last star fades out as the sun peeks over the horizon. The saltwater spray tickles her face. She licks her lips and notices they taste salty. She never tasted salt on her beach walks back home.

A starfish washes up by her toes. A little farther, she spies a sand dollar and several shells. Jade puts the starfish, sand dollar, and many beautiful shells in a bucket. She has never found these saltwater beauties on her freshwater beach.

She sits down on the shell-crushed sand and lets the water lap at her feet. She can't wait to see what she will find during her seven-day stay. Jade's heartbeat quickens as she sees dolphin fins cutting the surface of the water. She jumps up to get a better look.

Jade sees her mom and dad walking toward her. Mom calls that it is time to eat. Jade waves, then runs to her parents. They leave the warming beach. Breakfast is waiting in the cottage.

☞ Circle answers and follow directions.

1. What time of the day is it?   dawn   noon   afternoon   evening
   Highlight clues that helped you decide.

2. Where could Jade be?   Florida   Michigan   Arizona
   What made you choose this state? _____

   _____

3. How long will Jade be at this cottage?
        a day   a week   a month   a year

4. How does Jade feel about seeing the dolphins?   excited   bored   angry

5. Choose two words that describe Jade: sad   curious   happy   bored

Name _____

Kali and Koko

It was dusk. The blue-black sky was star-sprinkled and clear. Kali and Koko raced down the path. Jenny put the horses into the warm, musky barn, then turned to call her two companions.

She heard excited barking where the path met the woods at the far corner of the property. She leaned against the fence and called again. The only response was far-off barking. They've cornered something, she thought. "Kali! Koko! NOW!" Jenny warned.

She heard two yelps and then silence. Slowly, a strong, recognizable stench wafted through the air. Jenny's eyes began to burn and she held her nose. She jumped the fence quickly as the two hairy animals ran toward her.

"You two!" she groaned. "It looks like you've earned yourselves a few days out in the fresh air."

1. What are Kali and Koko? _____
   Highlight words or phrases that tell you this.

2. Why did Jenny jump the fence? _____
   _____
   Highlight words or phrases that tell you this.

3. What happened to Kali and Koko? _____
   _____
   What details helped you decide? _____
   _____
   _____

Name _____

It's That Time

Sally and Ned are swaying slowly in the family swing. The air is crisp. Sally puts her arm around Ned and snuggles into his shaggy body. Ned's tongue licks her hand that lies on her blue-jeaned leg. They watch a sluggish ladybug crawl underneath a pile of old, brown leaves. One red leaf drifts to the top of the ladybug's leaf pile. Ned's graying ears prick up as a southbound V of geese honks good-bye. The sky slowly turns from blue, to pink, to purple, to black.

The first star shines as Sally's mom calls them in to eat. Sally gives a last push as she slides out of the swing. She walks to the back door of the house. Ned leaps down. He barks once at a rabbit, then lopes after Sally. She smiles and rubs Ned's head as they walk into the warm house together.

☞ Circle answers and highlight in the text where you found the information.

1. What time of year is it?   summer   autumn   winter   spring

2. What time of the day is it? morning   afternoon   evening   night

3. What meal is Sally's family going to eat?   breakfast   lunch   supper

4. Where could this occur?   Florida   Hawaii   Wisconsin
   What made you choose this state? _____

   _____

5. How does Sally feel?   excited   peaceful   angry   ashamed

6. Who is Ned? _____

7. Sketch a picture of Ned in the picture frame above.

Figure It Out

☞ An idiom is a figure of speech. An idiom phrase means something different than what the words actually say. After each sentence, put an X in front of the best meaning for the underlined idiom phrase.

1. Gina has a beautiful flower garden. It seems like everything she plants grows. She really has <u>a green thumb</u>.
   ____ Gina's thumb is green in color.
   ____ Gina is a good gardener.
   ____ Gina has a green leaf wrapped around her thumb.

2. The storm came quickly and the rain poured down hard. Soon three inches of rain had fallen. Tom said it was <u>raining cats and dogs</u>.
   ____ It was raining really hard.
   ____ Cats and dogs were running around in the rain.
   ____ Cats and dogs were falling from the sky.

3. Pia and Tio have a new puppy. All day they chased him around the yard. They are ready to drop. The puppy <u>ran them ragged</u>.
   ____ The puppy tore their clothes into rags.
   ____ Pia and Tio used a rag to play with the puppy.
   ____ The puppy made Pia and Tio very tired.

4. Rita <u>couldn't keep a straight face</u>. The kittens were so funny. They chased each other's tails and got tangled up in Rita's shoelaces.

   ____ Rita couldn't look at the kittens.
   ____ Rita was angry at the kittens for scratching her face.
   ____ Rita just had to smile.

5. Kee had not done any extra reading at home. His reading scores were not improving. Kee wanted to become a better reader. He decided to <u>turn over a new leaf</u> and begin reading each day at home.

   ____ Kee will find a leaf and turn it over.
   ____ Kee will change what he is doing and make it better.
   ____ Kee will do a back flip by a tree.

Name _____

Chocolate Bars

Do you like to eat chocolate candy bars? Your parents may not let you eat chocolate very often, but long ago, many children did not get to eat chocolate at all. In fact, before the 1900s, most Americans had never tasted chocolate.

In ancient times, as early as 1000 BC, people enjoyed chocolate in a drink. It was made from cocoa beans and spices. It was very bitter. Through time, people learned to add sugar to make the drink sweeter. It wasn't until 1828 that a Dutch chemist found a way to make the fine powder we know as cocoa. Soon, candy makers began to find ways to make candy from cocoa.

In 1875, Daniel Peter of the Swiss General Chocolate Company and Henri Nestlé found a way to produce milk chocolate. Making the milk chocolate took a lot of work and was very expensive. It also took a long time; it took a whole week to make one batch of milk chocolate. People loved the milk chocolate. Some people used it as a medicine for mental stress, sickness, and weakness.

In the early 1900s, Milton Hershey found a way to mass produce milk chocolate, or make it in large amounts in a factory. He made the Hershey bars in his factory in Hershey, Pennsylvania. Mr. Hershey wanted everyone to be able to enjoy chocolate, so he sold his chocolate bars for five cents each. This was the first time most people could afford to eat and enjoy chocolate.

Thanks to these early scientists, and the candy makers of today, we have been enjoying milk chocolate in many kinds of candy bars.

☞ Sequence the following events.

____ Milton Hershey sold Hershey bars for 5¢ each.

____ People made a bitter drink from chocolate.

____ You can enjoy a chocolate candy bar.

____ Hershey developed a way to mass produce milk chocolate.

____ Peter and Nestlé found a way to produce milk chocolate.

____ A Dutch chemist found a way to make cocoa powder.

Name _____

☞ Read the article and complete the following.

1. Use one word to name the topic of this article. _____
   Highlight with red the first time you found this word in the article.

2. Why do you think that most children did not get to eat milk chocolate before the early 1900s? _____

   _____

   _____

   Highlight in yellow details that helped you decide this.

3. Do you think the milk chocolate made by Peter and Nestlé was expensive or

   inexpensive? _____

   What evidence does the article give to support your answer?

   _____

   _____

4. What is the definition of *mass produce* in this article? _____

   _____

   Highlight in green where you found the answer.

5. Why was Milton Hershey important to the history of milk chocolate? _____

   _____

   _____

   Highlight in blue the details that helped you decide this.

6. Were chocolate candy bars available in 1000 BC? _____

   What evidence does the article give to support your answer? _____

   _____

   _____

7. What is your favorite candy bar? _____
   Where did you get the last answer?   in the article   in my head

Ralph

Ralph was a dirty mutt. His once-white hair was gray and brown with grime. He wore a black collar around his neck that had once been blue. On the dirty collar hung an identification tag, if anyone could get close enough to read it.

Right now, Ralph was on his belly. He inched forward under the lilac bushes. His long hair dragged in the dirt. His bright, black eyes were glued on a plate at the edge of the table. On it was a ham sandwich. His moist, black nose twitched with the smell. Ralph knew he would get a swat with the broom or spray with the hose if the lady of the house caught him in the yard again.

His empty belly made him brave. The screen door slammed as the lady went back for other goodies. Ralph knew

it was time. He flew like a bullet to the edge of the table. The corner of the plate was in his mouth long enough to tip it onto the ground. Ralph's teeth seized the sandwich and he was off. The door slammed and a yell was heard. As he dove through a hole in the bushes, water from the hose whitened the back half of his body and his dirty tail.

1. What is Ralph? _____
    Highlight in yellow details that helped you decide this.

2. Is Ralph living in a home with people the day he steals the sandwich? _____
    Highlight in blue details that helped you decide this.

3. Did Ralph have a home with people at one time? _____

    _____

    Highlight in green details that helped you decide this.

4. How does the lady in the passage feel about Ralph? _____

    What details cause you to think this? _____

    _____

5. Draw Ralph in the frame above. Each time you draw a detail, highlight it in the text.

What Happens Next?

☞ Read each paragraph. Predict what will happen next by placing an X in front of the best answer. Highlight the clues in the paragraph that helped you decide what would happen next.

Pete ran into the kitchen to get a drink of water. He spied his jar of marbles sitting open on the kitchen table. Pete slipped on some water spilled on the floor. Pete's arm crashed into the table and upset the marble jar.

1. ___ The dog will bark.
   ___ The marbles will roll off the table and onto the floor.
   ___ His dad will yell at him.

Zoe's class has a math assignment of 25 problems. Their teacher said the assignment must be finished before each student can go out to recess. Zoe went to the bathroom, then talked to her friend. She had just finished the first five problems when the bell rang.

2. ___ Zoe will stay in and finish her math.
   ___ Zoe will go out to recess.
   ___ Zoe will do her spelling assignment.

Jeryl is crying. She fell on their driveway when her inline skates hit a stone. Her right knee is cut and blood is dripping down her leg. "Mom!" she calls. Jeryl's mother comes out of the house and runs to Jeryl, "Oh honey, let's go into the house and take care of that."

3. ___ Her mom will go skating with her.
   ___ Jeryl will throw her skates in the trash.
   ___ Jeryl's mom will help her wash her knee.

Evan loves to read books about insects. His class is in the library. He looks in the area where the insect books are usually found. None are there. One of the classes has checked out all the insect books for reports. He walks to the librarian.

4. ___ Evan will check out a book about cars.
   ___ Evan will ask the librarian if any insect books have been returned.
   ___ Evan will sit and draw insects.

Name _____

Venus Flytrap

Kayla got a Venus flytrap for her birthday. She put it with her other plants on her windowsill. She watered all of her plants each day.

After a week, all of her plants looked fine except her gift. She decided that she needed more information on this plant, so she went to the library and found a book about the Venus flytrap.

She was surprised to find out that this plant was carnivorous, or meat-eating. No wonder it was not doing well! The book said that the Venus flytrap is a popular house plant. Each set of leaves stays open until an insect or piece of meat lands on the inside of the leaf. The two leaves close quickly, trapping the bait inside. After a leaf digests the meat, it dies. A new leaf grows to take the place of the dead leaf.

Now Kayla knows how to take care of her Venus flytrap.

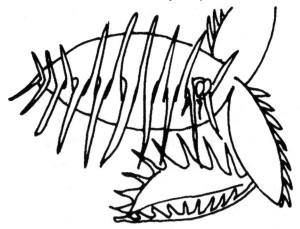

1. What kind of plant did Kayla get for her birthday? _____

2. Why did Kayla decide to go to the library? _____

    _____

3. What information about the plant surprised Kayla? _____

    _____

4. What does the word carnivorous mean? _____

5. What do you predict Kayla will do next? Highlight important details in the text with yellow that helped you with your prediction.

    _____

    _____

    _____

Name _____

Cranberries

When you think of delicious berries, you probably think of strawberries, blueberries, and raspberries. You probably don't ever think to snack on cranberries. Cranberries are tart berries used in relishes, chutneys, and desserts. Cranberries also make a delicious juice that is very healthy. Years ago in America, people used cranberry juice for dying rugs and blankets.

Cranberries are grown in the United States. The two states that grow the most cranberries are Massachusetts and Wisconsin. Cranberries are grown in a bog, or a wet piece of land. The berries grow in the bogs on vines. When it is time to pick the cranberries, the farmer floods the vines with water. A beater machine then knocks the berries off the vines. Since the cranberries are hollow, they float on the water. Special rakes are used to push the berries onto conveyor belts. The belts move the berries from the flooded bogs onto a waiting truck.

The trucks bring the cranberries to processing plants where the berries are either packaged or made into a cranberry product for us to enjoy.

1. Which two states grow the most cranberries? _____

   _____

2. What did the early Americans use cranberries for? _____

   _____

3. Sequence the following statements.

   ____ The cranberries float on the water.

   ____ The conveyor belt moves the cranberries onto a truck.

   ____ The cranberries ripen on vines in a bog.

   ____ The farmer floods the bog.

   ____ The truck brings the cranberries to a processing plant.

   ____ Berries are knocked off the vines by a beater machine.

   ____ Rakes are used to push the cranberries onto a conveyor belt.

Honey

Honey is a bee who lives in a hive in the center of an oak tree. Her hive has more than 70,000 bees. Honey is a worker bee. The worker bees are all female and they each have a job to do. Some worker bees are nursemaids for the larvae. Other workers are cleaners. Some workers guard the entrance of the hive and some, like Honey, collect nectar from flowers.

Honey follows directions given by another bee to find nectar. Today a bee dances the directions to a blueberry patch. Honey takes off. She flies along a creek until she gets to a sugar maple. She turns and flies through a group of pines, beside a fallen oak, and over a field of clover. She passes seven large rocks, then goes under a vine, and finally reaches the blueberry patch.

The petals of the blueberry blossoms make a landing strip for Honey. They direct her to the nectar in the center. Honey sips the nectar from several blossoms. She stores the nectar in her honey sac. In the honey sack, the nectar mixes with her saliva. Honey retraces her flight back to the hive where she empties the liquid from her honey sac into the wax cells of the hive.

During the six weeks she is alive, Honey will return again and again to the blueberry field for more nectar. Before she dies, Honey will have made about one teaspoonful of honey to help feed the hive.

1. Name three jobs worker bees can have. _____

    _____

2. How much honey does a bee make during its lifetime? _____

3. How does a honeybee find a plant? _____

4. Number the following statements to put them in the correct sequence.

    ____ Honey gets directions to the blueberry patch.

    ____ Honey uses the petals of the flower for a landing strip.

    ____ Honey brings nectar back to the hive.

    ____ Honey stores nectar in her honey sac.

    ____ Honey flies along the creek until she gets to the sugar maple.

Name _____

Coins

Coins are made in factories called mints. The first mint in America was in Philadelphia. Plans for this mint were started by a resolution of Congress on April 2, 1792. The first coins struck, or made, in America were minted that same year. The first denomination was called a half-disme or half-dime. A year later, several other denominations of coins were struck, including the quarter-dollar, the disme or dime, the gold eagles (worth $10), and the copper cent.

It took a lot of work to mint coins. Before a coin could be manufactured, a die was made. In the late 1800s, these dies were cut by hand. First an exact drawing had to be made. Then the drawing was traced into wax. The wax was used as a pattern to form steel. Finally a die, or mold, was finished which could be used to strike coins. Since this work was done by hand, the coins had small differences each time a new die was made.

Today, coins are standardized. Although hundreds of dies are used each year to make a denomination of coin, each die is made from a master die. Machines and computers are also used in this process so that the minted coins look alike. The only differences are the dates and the location codes which show where each coin is made.

☞ Choose the best meaning by placing an X in the correct blank.

1. What is the meaning of the word *mint* as used in this article?
   ___ a piece of candy ___ a factory where coins are made ___ a lot of money

2. What is the meaning of the word *strike* as used in this article?
   ___ to cross out ___ to attack ___ to make by stamping

3. What is the meaning of the word *die* as used in this article?
   ___ a mold ___ to color with a stain or paint ___ to stop living

4. What is the meaning of the word *standardized* as used in this article?
   ___ original ___ the same every time ___ a flag

5. What is the meaning of the word *denomination* as used in this article?
   ___ having the same size and value ___ color ___ sharing the same beliefs

Water Cycle

Pitter and Patter are two drops of water. They are great friends who usually travel the water cycle together. One day, something happened in the middle of a puddle and the two were separated. Some time later, Pitter and Patter met up again in a cloud. After a joyful reunion, the two told their stories.

"You wouldn't believe it," said Patter. "One minute, I was with you in the puddle, and the next minute I was gone. . ."

A big, rough, pink tongue swooped down and picked Patter up. He figured out it was a dog's tongue. Patter went into a warm, dark place. Lots of other drops were there. Patter went into the stomach where he had to share space with some slimy dog food, green beans, a penny, and the end of an ice cream cone. It was quite a party atmosphere. He spent some time traveling through the dog's digestive system before he was left in some grass by the side of the road. The warm sun beat down on Patter and the other drops of water. Some of the drops soaked into the ground, but not Patter. Soon, he became heated and began his journey back up through the sky into the clouds. He and many other drops were getting

together forming the cloud when he had spotted Pitter.

". . .and that's what happened," said Patter. "What happened to you?"

"Well," answered Pitter, "we were talking, and when I turned around you were gone. I saw other drops racing into the ground and thought you had gone ahead so I quickly followed them."

Pitter went sliding down through sand and soil and between rocks until she fell into an underground river. There she met millions of other drops that were on an underground roller-coaster ride. They bumped against rocks and coaxed small pieces to join them on their trip. They swept along anyone who would come with them until they slowed and joined a Great Lake. Slowly, over time, Pitter worked her way up through the thermal layers of the lake until she found herself at the surface. The warm sun beat down on Pitter. Soon she became heated and began her journey back up through the sky into the cloud where she had found Patter.

While they were catching up, the cloud was changing. They saw a flash, then heard a low rumble.

"Let's go," said Pitter.

"See you in the puddle," said Patter.

Name _____

☞ Number the events in Pitter and Patter's adventures so they are in the correct sequence. One sentence does not belong in each list. Cross it out.

Patter

___ He began forming a cloud.

___ He saw an ice-cream cone.

___ A tongue licked him up.

___ He was left on the grass.

___ He soaked into the ground.

___ He went through the dog's digestive system.

___ He became heated.

Pitter

___ She went on an underground roller-coaster ride.

___ She traveled the lake's thermal layers.

___ She went up into the sky.

___ She became heated.

___ She saw a penny.

___ She slid down through the soil.

___ She joined a Great Lake

Pitter and Patter each traveled a different path. Some of their experiences were different and some were the same. Compare their experiences using the Venn diagram below.

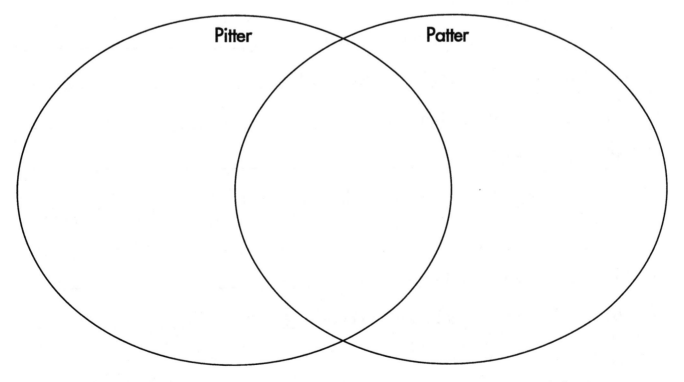

Northern Lights

You may see them in the north in the nighttime sky. They begin with a slight shimmer in the sky. Within minutes, thin poles of light are rippling across the sky. The lights are greenish or white in the center and slightly violet or red at the edges. They flow like a blanket being shaken out at the beach. They are known as the northern lights, or aurora borealis. They will take your breath away for ten to twenty minutes, then fade away.

The aurora borealis starts on our nearest star, the sun. On the sun, extremely hot gas particles are very excited. They create a state of matter, called plasma. This plasma escapes the sun's corona, or atmosphere. These particles, called a solar wind, spray out like water from a hose that someone swings in a circle over his head. The solar wind travels through space. If it is aimed at earth, it is attracted to the earth's magnetic field surrounding the north and south poles.

When this solar wind hits the earth's atmosphere, the particles strike atoms. These atoms release a burst of color. The storm of particles hitting the atmosphere is called an aurora substorm. When the plasma particles stop striking, the brilliant light show, called the aurora borealis, stops.

1. What is another name for the northern lights? _____

2. How long do the northern lights usually last? _____

3. Where do the northern lights start? _____

4. What is a corona? _____

5. What does the solar wind spray out from the sun like? _____

_____

6. What is an aurora substorm? _____

7. What causes the aurora borealis to end? _____

Which Meaning?

☞ Write the letter of the best meaning of the underlined word in the blank before each sentence.

1. ___ The gardener planted the flowers in a <u>bed</u> that would get lots of sunshine.

2. ___ The <u>bed</u> of coals glowed orange and yellow in the darkness. It was perfect for roasting marshmallows.

3. ___ Terri jumped into <u>bed</u> and pulled the covers up to her chin. She curled

   up and began reading her book.

   A. a piece of furniture   B. a plot of ground   C. a flat layer
   used for sleeping   prepared for plants

4. ___ Nancy rounded third base and ran for home <u>plate</u>.

5. ___ Maclin took the photographic <u>plate</u> to the printer so the newspaper could be published.

6. ___ George put salad and a burger on his <u>plate</u>.

   A. a smooth, flat, thin   B. a dish to eat from   C. a square bag to
   piece of material   mark a place

7. ___ Please <u>match</u> the sentence with the best answer.

8. ___ The class was watching the tennis <u>match</u>.

9. ___ Gail lit the <u>match</u>. She used it to light the birthday candles.

   A. a contest   B. a small stick with a   C. put together into
                  flammable material   a pair
                  on the end used to
                  start a fire

A Switch Is a Switch

☞ Choose the best meaning for the underlined word as used in the sentence.

1. As Meg walked out of the room, she turned the <u>switch</u> to off and the light went out.

   ___ A. to change from one thing to another

   ___ B. something used to turn off and on lights

   ___ C. a slender, flexible rod or twig

2. Dad told the children that they should have <u>minded</u> him. If they had, the bikes would not have been stolen.

   ___ A. something you think with

   ___ B. to dig minerals out of the earth

   ___ C. to follow someone's directions

3. Jean carefully removed the wax from the <u>mold</u>. Each candle was shaped like a star.

   ___ A. a form for making something into a certain shape

   ___ B. a fuzzy growth

   ___ C. the surface of the earth

4. Alex moved the <u>dash</u> up and down. It became harder to move as the cream turned into butter.

   ___ A. a short line

   ___ B. to run very quickly

   ___ C. the handle of the butter churn

5. Mom put a little <u>pat</u> of butter on the side of the plate.

   ___ A. to gently pet or tap

   ___ B. someone's name

   ___ C. a small individual portion

6. Choose two underlined words and write them on the lines below. Then use them in sentences. Use different definitions than the ones used in the sentences above.

   _____   _____

   _____

   _____

Think About It

☞ Write *fact* or *opinion* before each statement. If it is an opinion statement, highlight the word or words that helped you decide it was an opinion.

1. _____ The Pilgrims worked so hard they deserved a feast.

2. _____ Dr. Maulana Karenga is the teacher who founded Kwanzaa.

3. _____ Hexagonal plates and stellar dendrites are different types of snowflakes.

4. _____ The "Star Spangled Banner" is a beautiful song.

5. _____ John Adams was the second president of the U.S.A.

6. _____ Right triangles are easy to make.

7. _____ A square is a type of rectangle.

8. _____ The Gateway Arch is the tallest memorial in the United States.

9. _____ Dr. Seuss wrote and illustrated more than 40 books.

10. _____ E.B. White was a great author.

11. _____ Jesse Owens won four gold medals in the 1936 Olympics.

12. _____ Cobbles are stones that are greater than 6.4 cm but less than 25.6 cm in diameter.

13. _____ Plants need light and water to grow.

14. _____ African violets are beautiful, but hard to keep alive inside.

15. _____ The life cycle of a frog is interesting.

16. _____ Graphs are easy to make and to read.

Animals on Parade

☞ Write *fact* or *opinion* before each statement. If it is an opinion statement, highlight the word or words that helped you decide it was an opinion.

1. _____ The cheetah, who can run up to 62 miles per hour, is the fastest land animal.

2. _____ I think the giraffe's neck is very interesting to study.

3. _____ Koalas are marsupials, not bears.

4. _____ Siberian tigers are the biggest of all cats.

5. _____ People should not kill elephants for their tusks.

6. _____ A manta ray may measure up to 19 feet long.

7. _____ The speckled moray eel is creepy.

8. _____ Foxes are sneaky and clever.

9. _____ Raising horses is fun.

10. _____ You should keep your fruit in the refrigerator to keep fruit flies away.

11. _____ The harlequin tuskfish is really a beautiful fish.

12. _____ A newborn fox weighs about 4 ounces.

13. _____ Spiders are disgusting.

14. _____ Trap-door spiders are harmless to human beings.

15. _____ Squirrel monkeys live in the tropical rain forests of Central America.

16. _____ The shells of soft-shelled turtles are made of thickened skin.

Sports Report

☞ Read this radio editorial titled "My View in Sports" by Jack Page, which aired Saturday morning.

Friday's game against the Wild Ones tallied up another loss for the pathetic Dogs. They were terrible. It was hard to tell if the players were basketball players or golfers. Kollie led his sad team against the Wild Ones. Kollie made a beautiful shot from half court to bring the Dog's score to 12 at the end of the exciting first quarter. Shepard scored four perfect three-pointers in the final quarter, but the Wild Ones were too far ahead. The previously winning dogs should quit turning tail and go on the attack if they have any hope of making the play-offs again this year.

The Mudpies and the Quicksanders played an outstanding game. It was difficult to tell which would find solid ground as the score teeter-tottered back and forth all game. The dependable Granite put the Quicksanders on top at the last second with a score of 77 to 78. He made an awesome dunk just before the buzzer went off.

Across town, the fabulous Kilometers outdistanced the Miles with a final score of 86-68. The lightning bolt known as Decka scored half of the Kilometers' 86 points. This 6-foot-8-inch giant should go places. The Miles' two starting forwards, Van Inch and Mc Yard, were also impressive with 22 points each. Both of these blue-ribbon teams have a shot at this year's title.

The radio editorial is full of opinions. Reread the article and locate at least seven opinion words. Highlight them with yellow. Without using any of Mr. Page's opinion words, write three facts from each paragraph.

The game between the Dogs and the Wild Ones

_____

_____

The game between the Mudpies and the Quicksanders

_____

_____

The game between the Kilometers and the Miles

_____

_____

Packing

☞ Todd and his family are going to Florida on vacation. His mother gave him this list. He needs to make sure these items are in his suitcase. Compare the list to what he has already laid out for his suitcase.

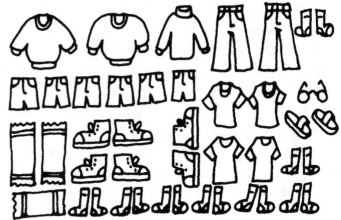

Todd,
2 sweatshirts
2 turtlenecks
2 pairs of jeans
4 pairs of shorts
5 short-sleeved shirts
5 pairs of underwear
2 pairs of pajamas
5 pairs of socks
1 spring jacket
1 toothbrush
1 pair of sunglasses
1 beach towel
1 pair of beach shoes
1 pair of tennis shoes

1. Highlight each item in the list that Todd has packed correctly. Name one item that Todd packed correctly.

_____

2. Name two items that Todd does not have laid out that his mother wants him to pack

_____

3. Name two items of which Todd has packed too many.

_____   _____

4. Name an item of which Todd needs more.   _____

5. How many more turtlenecks are needed? _____

6. How many more pairs of underwear are needed? _____

_____

7. Why is it important for Todd and his mother to plan ahead when packing for a trip?

_____

Two Events

☞ Henry brought these two notes home. Compare the notes and see the directions below.

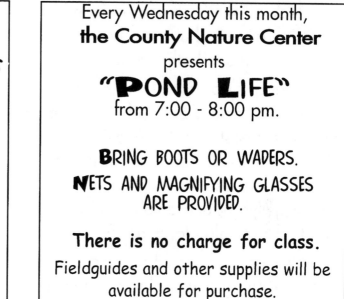

COME TO THE FAMILY FUN CARNIVAL!

GAMES   Saturday from 2:00-6:00   PRIZES
All Events are Free!
A brief outdoor program will
begin at 5:00. Program will include
music,
PIZZA   puppets, and a raffle!   POP

HAYRIDES

PONY RIDES   FACE PAINTING

PETTING ZOO

We hope you can come!
Sponsored by the Young Child Organization

Every Wednesday this month,
the County Nature Center
presents
"POND LIFE"
from 7:00 - 8:00 pm.

BRING BOOTS OR WADERS.
NETS AND MAGNIFYING GLASSES
ARE PROVIDED.

There is no charge for class.
Fieldguides and other supplies will be
available for purchase.

1. Circle the event that fits. You may circle both events.

Which event takes place outside?	Carnival	Pond Life
You can attend this event with no money.	Carnival	Pond Life
At which event will you see live animals?	Carnival	Pond Life
This event has a raffle.	Carnival	Pond Life

2. Which event asks participants to bring something? _____
   They are asked to bring _____ or _____
   Why do you think they are asked to bring it? _____

3. Henry's father promised to bring him to one event. His dad works weekends.
   Which event will they most likely attend? _____

4. Name one thing that is common to both events. _____

5. Write *T* if the statement is true. Write *F* if the statement is false.

   ____ There will be a petting zoo at the nature center program.

   ____ The carnival has free food.

   ____ A field guide can be purchased at the nature center.

   ____ A school is sponsoring both events.

Florida and Michigan

Michigan and Florida are both peninsula states. Each is surrounded by water on all sides but one. The water attracts tourists to both states.

Florida is bordered by saltwater. On the west side is the Gulf of Mexico and on the east side, the Atlantic Ocean. Different ocean creatures can be found in these waters, such as sharks, jellyfish, and dolphins. Guests can find seashells along the shores.

Michigan, on the other hand, is bordered by freshwater lakes. It touches four of the Great Lakes. Many freshwater fish, such as salmon and trout, swim in the lakes. Fishermen catch these and other fish. Guests love the sandy beaches and sand dunes.

Michigan and Florida are found in different parts of the United States. Florida is in the south. It is warm in Florida all year round. This allows farmers to grow crops such as oranges and coconuts. Michigan is found in the north. It has four seasons with great ranges in temperature. It is hot in the summer and cold and snowy in the winter. Autumn is a beautiful time in Michigan. In the autumn, the leaves on the trees change colors and then fall to the ground. Many fruits are grown in Michigan, such as blueberries, apples, cherries, and peaches.

☞ Compare the information about Florida and Michigan using the Venn diagram.

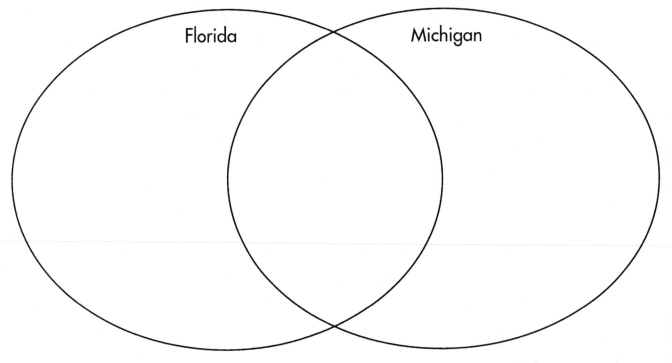

How Did It Happen?

☞ Read each event. Then write the missing cause or effect.

1. Judy and her dad made a bluebird house. They nailed it to a fence post in their backyard. Two bluebirds made a nest in the birdhouse.

   Cause: Judy and her dad made a birdhouse and put it in the backyard.

   Effect: _____

2. Toby left his new leather jacket outside. It rained. When Toby found his jacket the next day, the jacket was ruined.

   Cause: The jacket was left in the rain.

   Effect: _____

3. Jackie skipped breakfast. She went to school. By 10:30, she had a terrible stomachache.

   Cause: _____

   Effect: Jackie had a terrible stomachache.

4. Ernie came home from school. He saw his mom and gave her a huge hug. Ernie's mom smiled.

   Cause: Ernie gave his mom a hug.

   Effect: _____

5. There is a rule in Chambers' class that says, "If you don't get your work done during class time, you finish it at recess." Chambers has finished all of his work.

   Cause: Chambers has finished all of his work.

   Effect: _____

6. Mom was watching burgers frying on the stove. The baby started wailing. Mom went to see what was wrong with the baby. The burgers burned.

   Cause: The baby started wailing.

   Effect: _____

   Cause: _____

   Effect: The burgers burned.

Sand Dune

William climbed the huge sand dune. He was huffing and puffing just like the Big Bad Wolf by the time he reached the top. He flopped onto his back and closed his eyes to rest. After a few minutes in the warm sun, he jumped up and looked around. Then he walked to the edge of the dune. From the top of the hill, the autos looked like small toy cars. The people looked like insects. Taking one big, deep breath, William launched himself over the side. He ran as fast as he could. The sand sucked at his shoes. He pulled each leg up quickly so his feet would keep going faster than the rest of his body. He finally reached the bottom and sat down with a plop. He pulled off his tennis shoes and poured out a pile of sand. William grabbed his sister's hand and pulled her to the side of the hill to start the climb again.

☞ Choose the best answer and highlight the details in the story that helped you decide.

1. What caused William to huff and puff?

   ___ He had just read *The Three Little Pigs* and was practicing to be the wolf.

   ___ He had just climbed a sand dune and was tired.

   ___ He was huffing and puffing to tease his sister.

2. Why did the cars look like toy cars?

   ___ They were toy cars that William had brought along to play with.

   ___ William needed glasses to see better.

   ___ William was high up and the cars looked small because they were far away.

3. What caused the sand to be in William's shoes?

   ___ When he ran down the hill, the sand filled his shoes.

   ___ His sister filled his shoes with sand as a joke.

   ___ William didn't have sand in his shoes.

4. Why did William grab his sister's hand?

   ___ He wanted to get her back for putting sand in his shoes.

   ___ He had so much fun running down the hill, that he wanted her to have fun doing it, too.

   ___ He didn't want her to touch his toy cars.

Name _____

Coin Collecting

Numismatics, or coin collecting, is a very old hobby. It began long ago in other countries. It was not popular right away in America. Most Americans were too busy building a country out of a wilderness to think about collecting coins. It was not until about 1840 that Americans began to become serious coin collectors.

Coins are made in factories called mints. From 1792 to 1857, the United States made a cent coin that was as big as our current fifty-cent piece. In 1857, the United States stopped making the large-sized cent. When the big coins were hard to get, some people began the hobby of coin collecting.

Coin collecting became popular in the United States in the 1840s. Today, clubs are open to new coin collectors. There are many books and web sites about numismatics. You can also visit coin dealers for information and advice.

☞ Reread the article about coin collecting and complete the cause and effect chart below.

Cause	Effect
	Coin collecting was not popular in the United States before 1840.
	Many people began collecting the large-sized cent.
	Today you can buy coin collecting books and join numismatics clubs.

What a Disaster!

Nell is in a hurry. She forgot to set her alarm last night so it did not wake her up in time this morning. Now she is late for class, so she is racing down the hall. Nell flies around the corner and crashes into Chris. Chris was carrying his science project carefully to the classroom. He worked on it for three weeks. It was very well done. Chris's project falls to the floor. Chris bends down to pick up his things. He slips on the liquid from the project. As Chris falls, he grabs Nell's leg to steady himself. Nell falls too. This makes a terrible racket. A teacher comes into the hallway to see what is happening. Nell has twisted her ankle. The teacher sends her to the nurse and tells her to report to the office when she is done. Chris's project is a total disaster. The teacher sends him to the janitor's office to get help cleaning up.

☞ Refer to the article to complete the following.

1. What event started everything and caused all of the other events to happen?

_____

_____

2. What is your advice for Nell the next time she is late?

_____

_____

3. Give two possible effects of Chris's project getting ruined.

_____

_____

Name _____

☞ Reread the paragraph on page 68. Use the information to write the missing cause or effect. Then answer the questions below. Remember, an effect can also be a cause for a new effect.

Cause	Effect
	Nell's alarm didn't go off.
	Nell races down the hallway.
Nell crashes into Chris.	
Chris' project falls onto the floor.	
	Chris falls.
	Nell falls.
There is a terrible racket.	
	Nell goes to the nurse.

The Storm

The wind howled and the rain beat down. Lightning blazed with a quick light. Thunder crashed. The storm knocked down a towering oak down the street. It knocked out the electricity for the entire street. Willie sat in front of the dark TV set. He found a flashlight and turned it on.

Willie shone the flashlight ahead of him as he walked down the hallway. As he entered the kitchen, the flashlight batteries died. The room became inky black. Willie ran into the wall and stubbed his toe. He hollered and jumped on one foot. He bumped into the table, which upset his marble jar. The jar fell over. The marbles scattered all over the table and floor.

Willie's dog, Muttsie, jumped up at the noise and ran towards Willie's voice.

Muttsie skidded on the marbles. She flew across the floor into her dog dishes, spilling water and food all over.

The cat, Kitty, was showered with water. She jumped to the safety of the counter. She landed on the edge of a cookie sheet sticking out of the dish rack. The cookie sheet flipped over, taking the contents of the dish rack with it. The pots, plates, and silverware made an awful racket as they hit the floor. One of the pans struck the flour canister. The flour poofed up, covering everything in white.

Willie's mother heard the noise and came running with another flashlight. Amazed, she walked into the kitchen and stopped. "What happened here?" she asked.

Name _____

☞ Draw a picture showing one cause with its effect.

Fill in the blanks of the cause and effect chart. Remember, an effect can also be a cause for a new effect. The events are not in order.

Cause	Effect
The storm blew down the oak tree.	
	The TV was dark.
Kitty got wet.	
	Muttsie jumped up.
The pots, pans, and silverware fell.	
	Willie stubbed his toe on the wall.
Willie bumped into the table.	
	The cookie sheet tipped over the dish rack.
	Muttsie skidded on the floor.
The flour poofed up.	
	Mom came into the room.

Commercials

Television commercials catch our eyes. They can be entertaining and thought-provoking. They can make you laugh or cry. They can make you happy, excited, or even angry. Some are even better than the television programs they interrupt. Commercials may stay in our minds for days, months, or even years.

Companies pay large amounts of money to put commercials on television. Why do they pay? They want to sell us something. The purpose of a commercial is to make us believe that we need whatever it is selling— a toy, a pizza, or maybe a trip. Commercial makers are very good at convincing you.

Don't let the commercial convince you of something that is not true! After you watch a commercial, you should think about it. Decide what the commercial is trying to sell you. Decide whether this is something you want. Decide whether you really need it. Ask yourself if it is worth the money. Finally, decide whether you will be as happy with it when you get it home as the commercial makes you think. You must be careful not to let the commercial tell you what you want and need.

The next time you feel a commercial triggering your "need button," think about its purpose. If you cannot say no to commercials, perhaps the off button is the one you should push!

☞ Think about what you just read and answer the questions.

1. What is the author's purpose? _____

   _____

   Highlight details that helped you decide this.

2. What are some good things about commercials? _____

3. What might be bad about commercials? _____

   _____

4. What is a "need button"? _____

5. What is an "off button"? _____

6. Think of something you bought after seeing a commercial. What was it?

   _____

   Was it something you wanted before seeing the commercial? _____

   Did you need it? _____

   Was it worth the money? _____

   Was another brand available? _____

   Was it really as good as the commercial made it seem? Explain. _____

   _____

7. After reading this article, will you look at commercials differently? Explain.

   _____

   _____

Tall Tales

☞ Some authors stretch the truth to make the writing more interesting. Read the following passages. Put an X in front of the ones that could not be true. Highlight the fantastic parts with yellow.

____1. One day, Kim walked to school. On the way to school she saw a purple dog flying over the treetops.

____2. Rita is working on the computer. She is using the Internet to look for information about plants.

____3. Troy and his friends are at the swimming pool. They like to swim on hot summer days.

____4. Max picked another quarter from the vine and put it in his basket. His money plants were going to make him rich.

____5. Yanni's desk is at the front of the row. The row stretches from the South Pole to the North Pole.

____6. Ida felt the lump in her pocket all afternoon. She couldn't wait to get out of school so she could chew her bubblegum.

____7. A little nose poked its way out of Jason's backpack. Jason warned the alien to get back inside before someone saw it.

____8. Nan loved soccer. Her team was ahead in the finals. The score was one million to zero.

Choose a passage from above that is not true. Change it to make it true.

_____

_____

Choose a passage above that is true. Change part of it to make it fantasy.

_____

_____

Name _____

Bees

Dear Isabel,

Do you remember the bees we saw last week? We were scared of them. They came by our fresh peach sundaes so we killed them.

I just learned something about bees in school today. Did you know that without bees we would not have all of the fruits, vegetables, and other plants that we have today? Bees help pollinate plants. This is important because if the plants are not pollinated, seeds are not made. If seeds are not made, new plants will not grow. I'd sure hate to give up juicy peaches, sweet cherries, and messy watermelon!

I learned that bees are in trouble. There is a tiny mite, a member of the spider family, that kills baby bees. Other bees are killed by pesticides, or chemicals used to kill bad insects. There used to be enough bees to pollinate farmers' crops. Now some farmers have to pay a beekeeper to bring thousands of bees to the field to pollinate the plants.

I think I am going to be more careful next time I see a bee. I know they are kind of scary, but they are also very good for our farmers. I'm sorry I talked you into killing those bees last week.

Sincerely,

Jade

1. What is the author's purpose? _____
   Highlight key details that helped you decide this.

2. What is the main idea of paragraph two? _____

   _____

   Write two supporting details here.

   _____

   _____

3. What is the main idea of paragraph three? _____

   _____

   Write two supporting details here.

   _____

Name _____

Visiting Grandparents

☞ George kept a daily log of his vacation. Read the entries from four days, then answer the questions.

Monday: I arrived at Grandma and Grandpa's house. It was after supper, but I was hungry. Gramps made me a ham sandwich with potato chips. I get a bedroom all to myself. It has a full-sized bed with a blue-and-red quilt. One whole wall is full of bookshelves with books. I can't wait to read some of them. Maybe Gram will let me take some home with me. I can see a pond from the window. I wonder if there are any fish in it?

Tuesday: After breakfast, Gram took me to the pond. It is full of fish. We fed them bread crumbs and left-over pancakes. The fish eat more pancakes than I do! Too bad they couldn't enjoy Gramps's homemade maple syrup. A family of ducks came and ate too. One duck even took bread out of my hand.

Wednesday: We went shopping.

Thursday: Grandma and Grandpa took me to see the caves. They were really cool. In fact the temperature was cool too—ha, ha. It was really dark in the caves. We had to wear hats with lights on them. In the caves were gigantic stalactites and stalagmites. In one of the underground pools I saw fish without eyes. I bought a postcard about the blind fish to send to Mom and Dad.

You can often tell how the author feels about something by how he presents the information. The amount of writing and description helps you understand the author's viewpoint.

1. Name one activity George did not care for. _____

   How can you tell he didn't like this activity? _____

   _____

2. Name an activity George liked. _____

   What makes you believe George liked this activity? _____

   _____

3. Name another activity George liked. _____

   What makes you believe George liked this activity? _____

   _____

Reading Goals

☞ Mrs. Wallaker's students each filled out a reading goal sheet in September. In January, the students reviewed their goals and evaluated how they did. They each wrote a summary for their parents.

Here is Maddie's goal sheet from September:

> Goal: My reading level is 2.5.
>   I would like to be reading at 3.5 by January.
>
> My plan to reach my goal:
>   1.   I need to read at home 15 minutes before school.
>   2.   I need to read at home 20 minutes after school.
>   3.   I need to pay attention during reading.
>   4.   I need to make sure what I read makes sense.

This is what Maddie wrote as her evaluation:

> I know I met my goal because I am now reading at level 3.75. I met my goal because I made a chart on a calendar and kept track of my reading. I read every day before school except the week I was sick. I did read at least 20 minutes every day after school. I borrowed books at my reading level from my teacher and practiced them at school and at home. I paid attention when I read and made sure what I read made sense. When it did not make sense, I read it again. I always paid attention during reading in class. I know I am doing better in reading because I can read harder books and because I really like reading now.

1. Based on her evaluation, how does Maddie feel about her goal? _____

    Give evidence to support your answer. _____

2. How does Maddie's plan compare with her evaluation? _____

    _____

3. Name three things Maddie stated in her evaluation that helped her reach her goal.

    _____

    _____

Name _____

Puzzles

Today Jade, Will, Tony, and I cleaned up our classroom. We had indoor recess because it was raining outside. Boy, did everyone make a mess! Tanner had finished a puzzle, then left it on the counter. Then he played a game of checkers with Brian and left for the bathroom. We picked up the puzzle for him. Then we washed the counter. That counter was very dirty! It sure looked nice when we were done.

When Tanner came back, he was angry. He said he had wanted to show the puzzle to teacher. I told him he should have picked it up or told everyone he was going to take care of it later. He shoved me. One of the recess supervisors saw him do it and made him sit in his seat for the rest of recess.

After the counter, we cleaned up the sink area, the recess cupboard, the book area, and the math shelves. The room just sparkled. I think we did a better job than the janitor does! Our teacher was sure impressed. She said we could be the official class cleaners.

☞ An author's opinions and feelings are usually shown in the way she presents the information.

1. How does the author feel about cleaning up the room? _____

_____

Highlight details that make you believe this.

2. Does the author believe putting away the puzzle was right or wrong?

_____

What does she write that makes you believe this? _____

_____

3. Does Tanner believe putting away the puzzle was right or wrong? _____

What makes you believe this? _____

_____

Pencils

☞ Mrs. William's class needs to buy new pencils. They decided to test four different kinds. They recorded their findings in a chart.

Brand	Lasted for one week or longer	Kept a sharp point	Eraser lasted for one week or longer	Eraser worked well
Brand A	no	no	yes	no
Brand B	yes	yes	no	yes
Brand C	no	yes	no	yes
Brand D	yes	yes	yes	no

Refer to the information in the chart to put a *T* in front of the true statements and an *F* in front of the false statements.

1. ____ Brand B lasts longer than Brand A.

2. ____ Brand C, Brand D, and Brand A all kept a sharp point.

3. ____ The eraser on Brand A did not last as long as the eraser on Brand C.

4. ____ The eraser worked well on all four brands.

5. ____ The lead did not keep a sharp point on one of the brands.

6. ____ Brand A did not work well in any of the areas.

7. ____ Brand C kept a sharp point, but it did not last one week.

8. ____ Brand D has an eraser that worked very well.

9. ____ Brand B would be a good choice if you wanted an eraser to last longer than one week.

Which pencil would you recommend the class buy? _____

Use the information given in the chart to support your choice. _____

Name _____

Letter to Grandma

Dear Grandma,

I am glad that you are having a good time on the beach. I'll bet it is warm there. Are you too hot? Do you have to use fans and an air conditioner? I can't wait to get there during spring vacation. I want to go fishing with you and grandpa and swim and pick up shells and walk on the beach.

It is snowing like crazy here. Don't tell my mom I am telling you, but Mom cracked up the car yesterday. Some guy crashed right into the back of the car. It was just too icy. Mom was really upset. She even "cooked" at a restaurant on the way home. I hope she will pick up take-out food more often, even if the car is OK.

I had fun in the snow. We have a huge sledding hill. Meg and I went down it over and over. We made a family of snowmen too. Then we got cold. My fingers and toes felt like they were going to fall right off! My snow pants were soaked right through and my nose and cheeks were redder than all get out.

Hey, is your nose red? Are you wearing sunscreen on your face? Remember when you made me put some on and I cried because I was so little. I think Meg cried more than I did.

I sure miss you. I will see you soon.

Love,

Ian

☞ You can tell quite a bit about how an author feels about things by the way he writes about them. Refer to the letter to complete the following.

1. How does the author feel about how things are going where he lives?
List two good things and two negative things about home.

         good   negative

_____   _____

_____   _____

2. What did Ian mean when he said his mother "cooked" at a restaurant?

_____

_____

What words told you that? _____

Does the author like it when his mom "cooks at a restaurant"? _____

_____

_____

3. How does Ian feel about where his grandma is?
List two good things and two negative things about Grandma's home.

         good   negative

_____   _____

_____   _____

The Summer House

Ernie and his family drove around the lake. The road cut through the forest. Ernie could just see the ice blue water through the maples, oaks, and pines. He couldn't wait to go for a swim. Squirrels and other quick animals darted through the trees as the car approached them. Birds called back and forth announcing their arrival at the summer house.

The sun was directly overhead when they pulled into the driveway. Ernie could see the yard needed mowing. It was hard to find grass in all the weeds. He hoped his parents wouldn't mow right away. He could see interesting insects and butterflies flying from wildflower to wildflower. Ernie had brought his bug jar and butterfly net. It looked like he would have lots of insects to add to his collection.

In the middle of the sunny clearing stood the house Ernie's family had rented for the summer. The blue house was two stories tall. Right in the middle of the bottom floor was a doublewide, bright-red

door. Upstairs, there were two large, rectangular windows located on each side of the downstairs door. The two windows looked like big, dark eyes. Ernie hoped he could have the room on the left. The branch of an old oak tree reached right under the window. Ernie thought of using it as a way out of his room.

The paint on the house, which had once been blue, was peeling off and looked gray. The roof was jet black, soaking up the heat from the sun. There must have been windows on the first floor, but you couldn't see them hidden behind the overgrown bushes and the large screened porch. Many holes were rusted through the screen and it was covered with vines, which grew as tall as the second floor. Ernie thought the porch would be a great place to make a fort.

Ernie's parents groaned. Ernie stared wide-eyed at the house. This place was going be quite a summer experience.

Name _____

☞ Ernie and his parents don't seem to agree about the summer house. Ernie thinks it will be a wonderful place. His parents groan. Write about their different viewpoints.

1. How do they view the yard?

    Ernie's parents see _____ and it makes them think of

    _____ .

    Ernie sees _____ and it make him think of

    _____ .

2. How do they view the house?

    Ernie's parents see _____ and makes them think of

    _____ .

    Ernie sees _____ and it make him think of

    _____ .

    Ernie's parents see _____ and makes them think of

    _____ .

    Ernie sees _____ and it make him think of

    _____ .

3. Draw a picture of the summer house. Each time you use a detail from the text, highlight it with yellow. Include as many details as you can.

Name _____

Vertebrates

☞ Vertebrates are animals with backbones. They can be sorted into different categories. This table shows the characteristics of five kinds of vertebrate. Use the chart to answer the questions.

Class	Amphibian	Bird	Fish	Reptile	Mammal
Body covering	skin	feathers	scales	scales	skin and hair
Birth	egg	egg	egg	egg	live
Drinks mother's milk	no	no	no	no	yes
Warm or cold-blooded	cold	warm	cold	cold	warm
Breathes with gills or lungs	gills when young, lungs when adult	lungs	gills	lungs	lungs

1. Are amphibians warm- or cold-blooded? _____

2. Which kind of vertebrate drinks its mother's milk? _____

3. Which vertebrate breathes with gills its whole life? _____

4. What is the body covering of a bird? _____

5. Give two reasons why humans must be mammals. _____

_____

6. According to the chart, what do amphibians, fish, and reptiles have in common?

_____

Name _____

Beverages

Food labels provide a lot of information. They tell how healthy a food is, how many calories are in the food, and what it is made of. The ingredients are listed in order from greatest to least. So, if sugar is listed as the first ingredient, there is more sugar in the food than any other ingredient.

Sugar is found in many foods and drinks. You may not always know sugar is there because it has many names on food labels. Some other words for sugar are fructose, sucrose, dextrose, and corn syrup.

Madalen made the chart below with information from the labels of five drinks she found in her house.

Beverage	1st Ingredient	2nd Ingredient	3rd Ingredient	Calories per 8 oz.
A.	filtered water	corn syrup	orange juice	120
B.	sucrose	dextrose	citric acid	60
C.	sugar	dairy whey	corn syrup	140
D.	filtered water	high-fructose corn syrup	raspberry juice	140
E.	carbonated water	high-fructose corn syrup	citric acid	100

1. Circle all words for sugar in the chart. How many did you circle? _____

2. Use the information in the chart to put a T in front of the true statements and an F in front of the false statements.

_____ All five beverages have sugar as one of the first three ingredients.

_____ Drinks A, B, D, and E do not include sugar as its first ingredient.

_____ Drinks C and D have the same number of calories per 8 ounces.

_____ The first three ingredients in drinks D, C, and E are sugar.

_____ High-fructose corn syrup is another name for sugar.

Home Runs

In one year, two players broke a baseball record made 37 years before. In 1998, Sammy Sosa and Mark McGwire both beat the record for the greatest number of home runs in one baseball season. This record was originally held by Babe Ruth who had 60 home runs in 1927. Then Roger Maris broke Ruth's record in 1961 with 61 home runs. Sammy Sosa, who played for the Chicago Cubs, had 66 home runs. Mark McGwire, who played for the St. Louis Cardinals, finished the season with 70 home runs. Mark McGwire now holds the record.

For the entire 1998 season, fans watched the statistics to see which one of these players would first break the record made by Roger Maris. Once the record was broken by both players, it was a race to see who would hold the new record.

☞ The table shows how many home runs Sammy Sosa and Mark McGwire made each month of the 1998 season.

Player	March	April	May	June	July	August	September
McGwire	1	10	16	10	8	10	15
Sosa	0	6	7	20	9	13	11

Answer the questions. Then circle where you found the answer.

1. Who first held the record for home runs in one season?_____
   in the text   in the chart   both

2. Who held the record at the end of 1961? _____
   in the text   in the chart   both

3. At the end of 1998, who held the record for home runs? _____
   in the text   in the chart   both

4. Who had the most home runs in June of 1998? _____
   in the text   in the chart   both

5. Which month did Sammy Sosa beat Roger Maris's record? _____
   in the text   in the chart   both

6. Did Mark McGwire beat the old record and gain the title in the same month or different months? Which month(s)? _____
   in the text   in the chart   both

Insect Report

Ian presented a report about the importance of insects. He included information about how insects pollinate plants. He listed products we use that depend on insect pollination, such as cotton blue jeans, jack-o-lanterns, and apples. He told the class that in the last 10 years, we have lost about one-fourth of the insect pollinators. This is due to such things as wildflowers disappearing and pesticides being used. Ian also displayed step-by-step directions with photos showing how to build a bumblebee house. Ian wanted to know if his report could change how people felt about insects. He surveyed the class before and after his report. Here are the results of his surveys.

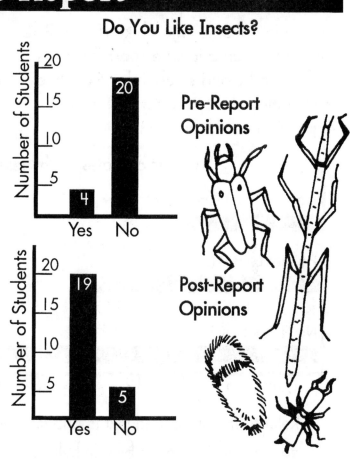

Do You Like Insects?

Pre-Report Opinions

Post-Report Opinions

☞ Refer to the graphs and text to answer the following questions. Circle where you found the answer: the text, the graphs, or both.

1. Do the students feel the same about insects before and after the report?

   _____

           in the text   in the graphs   or both

2. Why are insects important? _____

           in the text   in the graphs   or both

3. Compare the pre- and post-report graphs. Write two true statements about the graphs. Consider using words such as most, fewer, more than.

   _____

   _____

4. Highlight details in the report that may have caused the post-report opinions.

Bike Helmets

Many people enjoy bike riding. Bike riding is a fun and safe sport if cyclists follow traffic and safely rules. A helmet can protect the cyclist against head injuries in a bike accident.

By 1998, many cities and states realized the importance of helmets. Several states decided to pass a law requiring children to wear helmets when riding their bikes.

Number of States With Helmet Laws

Working on Helmet Law *

Helmet Law Passed **

No Helmet Law

0   3   6   9   12   15   18   21   24   27

*AZ, IL, KS, KY, MO, NC, NM, OH, SC

**AL, CA, CT, DE, FL, GA, MA, ME, NJ, NY, OR, PA, RI, TN, WV

☞ Refer to the graph and text to answer these questions.

1. How many states have bicycle-helmet laws? _____

2. How many states have no statewide helmet laws? _____

3. If each state that is working on a helmet law passed one, how many states would have helmet laws? _____

4. Does Wisconsin have a bicycle-helmet law? _____

   Where did you find the information to answer this question? _____

5. If you live in Indiana, where there is no law requiring you to wear a bicycle helmet, do you need to wear a helmet if you are on vacation in Florida? _____

6. Name six states that have bicycle-helmet laws. _____

   _____

7. Do you think there should be helmet laws? Explain your answer. _____

   _____

Name _____

Baseball

☞ Meg likes to graph the results of the weekly games in her baseball team's division. She placed the five teams with the most wins on a graph to share with the school newspaper. Use her graph to answer the questions.

◯ = two wins

Top Five Teams in Stanfield's Fifth Division	
Gizmos	◯ ◯ ◯ ◯ ◯
Spuds	◯ ◯ ◯ ◯ ◯ ◯ ◖
Microchips	◯ ◯ ◯ ◯ ◯ ◖
Space Cadets	◯ ◯ ◯ ◯ ◯ ◯
Kazoos	◯ ◯ ◯ ◯ ◯

1. Which team has won the most games? _____

2. How many games has this team won? _____

3. How many more wins do the Spuds have than the Gizmos? _____

4. What place are the Microchips in? _____

5. How many wins do the Space Cadets have? _____

6. Which two teams have an equal number of wins? _____

7. The team that is in last place is the Hurricanes. They have 3 wins. How many more wins would they need to catch up to the Kazoos? _____

Name _____

New Baby

☞ This is the table of contents for a book. Read the table of contents and answer the questions below.

1. On what page does "Maybe We Can Keep Her" start?

   _____

2. On what page does "Don't Touch My Stuff!" start?

   _____

3. Which chapter begins on page 14? _____

4. Which chapter begins on page 40? _____

5. Which chapter ends on page 59? _____

6. Which chapter ends on page 13? _____

Table of Contents
The New Baby.............................1
If I Were an Only Child.................14
A Trip to the Zoo..........................29
Two A.M. Crying...........................40
You Can Have Her; She's Free........47
Don't Touch My Stuff!.....................60
"Ga Ba Da Wa—Wov Oo"............72
Maybe We Can Keep Her.............83

7. How many pages in the chapter "If I Were an Only Child"? _____

8. How many chapters are in this book? _____

9. What is the title of the third chapter? _____

   On what page does this chapter begin? _____ End? _____

10. What is the title of the seventh chapter? _____

    On what page does this chapter begin? _____ End? _____

    How many pages are in this chapter? _____

11. What do you think would be a good title for this book? _____

    _____

Name _____

Science Book

☞ Read the table of contents and answer the questions below.

1. In which unit would you look if you wanted information about your inner ear? _____

2. If you were reading page 17, which would you be reading about?

   ___ the difference between a solid and a liquid

   ___ how a solid changes to a liquid

   Explain your choice. _____

   _____

3. If you want to know about diamonds, emeralds, coal, and sulfur, on what pages would you look?

   _____

4. If you were reading page 109, which you would be reading about?

   ____ the types of plants that thrive in the rainforest

   ____ how a seed grows into a seedling, then a plant which produces a seed

   Explain your choice. _____

5. If you are reading about how wind and water change rock formations, what unit and chapter are you reading? _____

Name _____

A Year in My Life

☞ This table of contents comes from a book titled *A Year in My Life*.

Refer to the table of contents for the book *A Year in My Life* to choose the correct response.

1. On what page does Chapter 9 begin?

  A.   229

  B.   101

  C.   156

  D.   can't tell from the information given

Name _____

2. On what page does Chapter 14 end?

    A.   246

    B.   259

    C.   262

    D.   can't tell from the information given

3. Which chapter starts on page 177?

    A.   Chapter 7 "Things Become Green"

    B.   Chapter 9 "School's Out"

    C.   Chapter 10 "Temperature Rising"

    D.   Chapter 14 "School Bells"

4. What is the title of Chapter 2?

    A.   "The House by the Lake"

    B.   "Halloween Party"

    C.   "Fishing"

    D.   "Swimming Holes and Sprinklers"

5. In which chapter do you think the children went tobogganing?

    A.   Chapter 2

    B.   Chapter 6

    C.   Chapter 7

    D.   Chapter 12

6. What time of year do you believe it is in Chapter 10?

    A.   Spring

    B.   Summer

    C.   Autumn

    D.   Winter

7. How many pages are in Chapter 6?

    A.   17

    B.   117

    C.   16

    D.   can't tell from the information given

Name _____

Nursery Rhyme Ads

☞ The following advertisements were found in a Nursery Rhyme Land newspaper. Each ad is missing important information. Fill in the information based on your knowledge of nursery rhymes.

Seeking job tasting pastry. Very good with plum pies. Call _____.	Looking for pickled pepper pickers. Need to be able to count the amount picked. For application, ask _____.
Mother seeking home with 70 bedrooms. Also looking for patient, reasonably-priced babysitter. Send inquiries to _____.	Shepherdess looking for an assistant. Needs someone very good at locating lost sheep. Apply in person to _____.
Brother and sister looking for qualified water carrier. Send replies to _____.	**BLACKBIRD PIE SALE!** Four-and-twenty birds **guaranteed** in each pie. Call king for details. Each pie is reasonably priced at _____.
Dog bone wanted for empty cupboard. Deliver to _____.	
Call immediately! Yolk looking for doctor able to reassemble bodies. Ask for: _____.	Seeking daytime job. Have good communication skills. Have experience running through the town in nightgown. Call _____.

Old Mother Hubbard   Little Miss Muffet   Peter Piper   Wee Willie Winkie

Little Jack Horner   Jack and Jill   Sixpence   Mary Had a Little Lamb

Jack Sprat   Humpty Dumpty   Little Boy Blue   Old Woman in Shoe

Name _____

Fairy Tale Headlines

☞ If fairy tales were real, how would the stories be reported in the newspaper? Here are some headlines to get you thinking. Which fairy tales do they represent?

Brick House Protects Against Lupine Invasion!

People Protest as Castle Orders 12 Pair of Dancing Slippers!

Giant Offers Reward For Poultry Thief !

Poison Apple Keeps Doctor Away Permanently!

Sleeping Princess Bring Castle Life to a Complete Halt!

Monster Wins Beauty's Hand in Marriage

The Three Little Pigs	Sleeping Beauty	Jack and the Beanstalk
Twelve Dancing Princesses	Snow White	Beauty and the Beast

Baby Book

☞ Maria was looking through her baby book. She discovered that her parents had completed a time line for her first year of life. Here is part of the time line.

Oct. 16   Maria Adriana; born at 2:06 p.m.; 8 pounds, 2 ounces; 21 inches

Nov. 16   one month old—can lift head when on tummy

Dec. 16   two months—smiles now; makes a cooing noise

Jan. 16   three months—laughs; brings hands together

Jan. 20   rolled over from tummy to back

Feb. 16   four months—rolls both ways from tummy to back; squeals; reaches for toys

Mar. 16   five months—rolls, keeps head steady; just starting to sit but needs support; says "da-da-da"

April 16   six months—sits by self; rolls across floor

May 16   seven months—picks up little things; gets upset when toy is taken away; reaches to get a toy she wants

June 16   eight months—can stand up holding on to something; plays peek-a-boo; gets into sitting position from tummy

June 30   first tooth came in today—in front, bottom right

July 16   nine months—pulls up and stands while holding onto furniture; started eating baby food—she likes carrots, but doesn't care for plums

1. How old was Maria when she started sitting by herself? _____

2. Which was Maria's first tooth? _____

    When did it come in? _____

3. What happened on January 20? _____

4. Was Maria able to sit by herself or squeal first? _____

5. When did Maria start eating solid foods? _____

    Which foods did she like and not like? _____

Family Tree

☞ A family tree is a diagram that shows relationships in a family. A horizontal tie is two people who get married. A tie going down the page is a child. Look at the family tree of Joe and Sue. It shows four generations of their family. Refer to the diagram to answer the questions below.

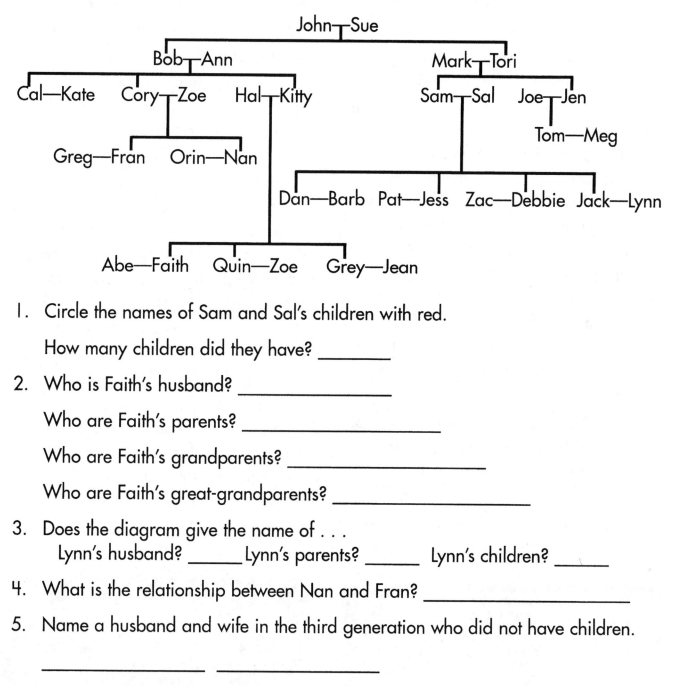

1. Circle the names of Sam and Sal's children with red.

   How many children did they have? _____

2. Who is Faith's husband? _____

   Who are Faith's parents? _____

   Who are Faith's grandparents? _____

   Who are Faith's great-grandparents? _____

3. Does the diagram give the name of . . .
   Lynn's husband? _____ Lynn's parents? _____ Lynn's children? _____

4. What is the relationship between Nan and Fran? _____

5. Name a husband and wife in the third generation who did not have children.

   _____ _____

6. Name two cousins. _____ _____

U.S. Paper Money

The United States has its own forms of money, different from all other countries. Money in the U.S. has changed over time and continues to change to meet the needs of the users.

In the United States, paper money was first issued in 1775. That year, the Continental Congress authorized the issue, or giving out, of paper money to finance the Revolutionary War. This "continental currency" soon came to be worth very little and fell out of use. In 1785, the U.S. government decided that the official money system would be based on the dollar. In the 1860s, the United States government issued paper money that looks much like the money we use today. The backs of these bills were printed with green ink. The green ink gave the bills the nickname "greenbacks."

In 1865, the Secret Service was established to control counterfeits, or fake money. At that time, about one-third of the money in circulation was counterfeit.

Paper bills feature important people from U.S. history. For example, the one-dollar bill has George Washington; the two-dollar bill has Thomas Jefferson; and the five-dollar bill has Abraham Lincoln. These three men also appear on coins.

Paper money was not always the size it is today. At one time, the bills were larger. In 1929, the bills were all made the same size, which is the size they are today.

In the 1990s, new security features were added to several bills to prevent counterfeiting. Some of these features include color-shifting ink, microprinting, and a security thread. The first bill to be changed was the 100-dollar bill in 1991.

By 1999, only the 1-, 2-, 5-, 10-, 20-, 50-, and 100-dollar bills were still produced, although bills of higher denominations were still in use. As new bills are made, the old are not immediately taken out of circulation. Paper bills are in constant use and will continue to be updated as the needs of the U.S. consumers change.

☞ Refer to the information on page 98 to complete this time line.

1700s   1775 1785   1800s   1860 1865   1900s   1929   1990 1999   2000

1. What is currency? _____

2. In what year was the U.S. Secret Service established? _____

   Why? _____

3. What does *issue* mean? _____

4. What gave paper money the nickname "greenbacks"? _____

   _____

5. Which three famous people appear on both bills and coins? _____

   _____

6. What year were all bills changed to one size? _____

7. Why were security features added to paper money in the 1990s? _____

   _____

Dolphins & Porpoises

Have you ever watched a trained dolphin at an aquarium or water park? Dolphins are believed to be among the smartest animals. There are many kinds of dolphins. The most familiar are the bottle-nosed and the common dolphin. The killer whale is actually considered a dolphin. Dolphins are closely related to both porpoises and whales. Whales are much larger than most dolphins and porpoises. The main differences between dolphins and porpoises are the shape of their heads and the size of their bodies.

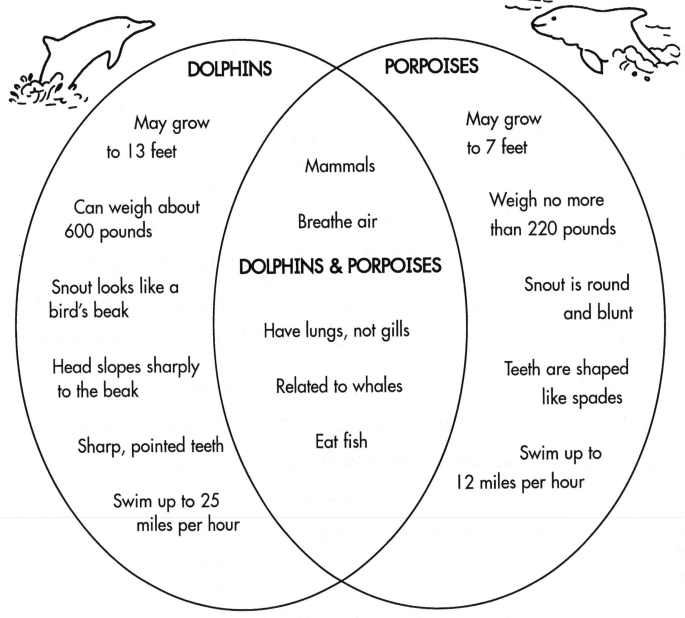

DOLPHINS

May grow
to 13 feet

Can weigh about
600 pounds

Snout looks like a
bird's beak

Head slopes sharply
to the beak

Sharp, pointed teeth

Swim up to 25
miles per hour

DOLPHINS & PORPOISES

Mammals

Breathe air

Have lungs, not gills

Related to whales

Eat fish

PORPOISES

May grow
to 7 feet

Weigh no more
than 220 pounds

Snout is round
and blunt

Teeth are shaped
like spades

Swim up to
12 miles per hour

Name _____

☞ Study the Venn diagram to compare the differences and similarities between porpoises and the most common species of dolphins. Use the information given in the
   Venn diagram to answer the questions below.

1. A mammal is swimming just in front of your boat. Your boat is traveling at 18

   miles per hour. Is it a dolphin or a porpoise? _____

   What information helped you make this decision? _____

   _____

2. An animal is swimming just offshore. You can see that it has a round, blunt

   snout. Is it a dolphin or a porpoise? _____

3. Name two things dolphins and porpoises have in common. _____

   _____

4. You see a creature that is 5 feet long swimming at 10 miles per hour. Why

   isn't this enough to tell you if it was a dolphin or a porpoise? _____

   _____

   What attribute could you look for to determine if the animal is a dolphin or a

   porpoise? _____

5. What does a dolphin eat? _____

6. Which animal has sharp, pointed teeth? _____

7. Which animal is generally smaller than the other? _____

Name _____

John Glenn

On November 5, 1998, Senator John Glenn traveled into space as the oldest astronaut ever. He was 77 years old.

This was not the first time John Glenn was in space. Years earlier, when he was 40 years old, John Glenn was the first American to circle the earth. During that trip in 1962, he traveled on the Friendship 7. He orbited, or went around, the earth three times. He was the only person on board the Friendship 7 and had only one window to look out. That space ship had no computers on board. John Glenn talked to people on earth while he was in space. They wanted to observe his reaction to the space environment.

In 1998, John Glenn went into space on the space shuttle Discovery. This time, he was not alone. There were six other astronauts on board the Discovery with him. The Discovery crew orbited the earth 144 times. They had ten windows to look out. They also had five computers helping them. This time, scientists wanted to observe the reaction of an older man in the space environment.

Glenn was an American hero in 1962 for orbiting the earth. John Glenn became a hero again in 1998 when he traveled as the oldest astronaut to orbit the earth.

1. Why was John Glenn a hero in 1962? _____

_____

2. Why was John Glenn a hero in 1998? _____

_____

3. What does *orbited* mean? _____

_____

Name _____

☞ In the article, highlight key facts about the 1962 flight with yellow. Highlight key facts about the 1998 flight with blue. Use the information to fill in the Venn diagram below. Write at least three facts for each year and three facts that the two flights share.

John Glenn's Space Flights

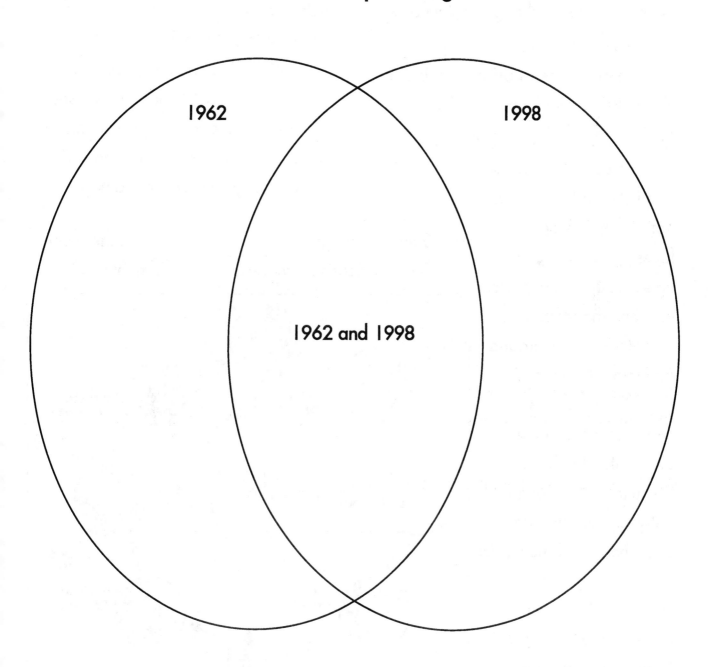

1962

1998

1962 and 1998

Name _____

The Moon and Its Phases

The moon seems to change each night when you look in the sky. It appears a little bigger or a little smaller than it did the night before. Actually, the moon doesn't change, just what we can see changes.

The moon seems bright, but it does not make its own light. The moon reflects the light from the sun.

The part of the moon that is lighted by the sun is not always the part that faces the earth. At all times, half the moon faces the sun. The moon is a satellite. It orbits around the earth. As it moves around, we see the parts that face the earth and are lighted by the sun. Sometimes the moon is between the earth and sun. Then all of the lighted part is facing away from the earth. The moon appears black to us. This is called the new moon.

The 29-day cycle of the moon's phases begins with the new moon. Each night after the new moon, more of the moon appears lighted. This part of the cycle is called waxing. When all of the lighted side of the moon faces the earth, it is called the full moon. This happens halfway through the phases of the cycle. As the moon cycle continues, we see less and less of the moon. This part of the cycle is called waning.

☞ Study the diagram of the eight phases of the moon. These phases repeat in a cycle each month.

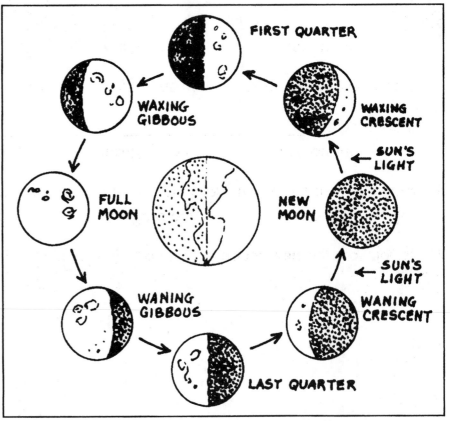

☞ Answer the following questions, then circle where you found the answers: the text, the diagram, or both.

1. Why do we see moonlight? _____

   _____
   in the text   in the diagram   or both

2. What does a waxing gibbous look like? _____
   in the text   in the diagram   or both

3. How many days are in a moon cycle? _____
   in the text   in the diagram   or both

4. What does the moon travel around? _____
   in the text   in the diagram   or both

5. Which phase in the cycle occurs opposite from the waning gibbous?

   _____
   in the text   in the diagram   or both

6. What is a satellite? _____
   in the text   in the diagram   or both

7. If the new moon happened on June 29, in which month would the next new

   moon occur? _____
   in the text   in the diagram   or both

8. How much of the moon faces the sun at any given time? _____
   in the text   in the diagram   or both

9. If you saw the new moon on January 1, which phase would you see on

   January 14 or 15? _____
   in the text   in the diagram   or both

10. How many phases are there in one cycle of the moon? _____
   in the text   in the diagram   or both

North and South Pole

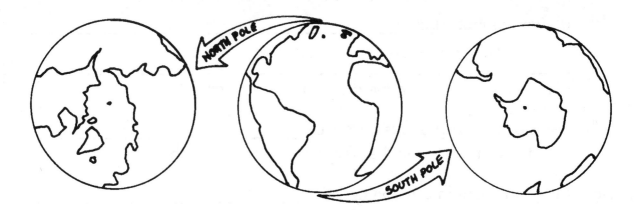

The North Pole and South Pole are on opposite ends of the earth. Both places are very cold and desolate. Although they are very far apart, they are alike in many ways.

The poles are located in different hemispheres. The North Pole is located at the northernmost point of the northern hemisphere. If you stand on the North Pole, every direction you turn is south. The South Pole is located at the southernmost point of the southern hemisphere. If you stand on the South Pole, every direction you turn is north.

The North Pole is located in the Arctic. The North Pole is covered with ice. Below the ice is the Arctic Ocean, not land. The South Pole is also covered in ice. Below the ice, however, is Antarctica. Antarctica is a land mass, which is the seventh continent. The land is covered with ice. Its deepest ice is over 15,000 feet (4,500 meters) deep.

Antarctica and the Arctic both have a summer and a winter. However, when Antarctica is having its summer, the Arctic is having its winter. During its summer, each place has sunlight for 24 hours. During its winter, each place has darkness for 24 hours.

No people live in either icy region surrounding the poles. The people who visit the poles are usually scientists, explorers, and athletes. Without special equipment, people cannot survive in either of these environments.

Some animals can survive the bitter cold. Seals live in both areas. They survive near the icy waters. Polar bears live only in the Arctic. Penguins live in Antarctica. Some penguins also live on the continents in the southern hemisphere, but no penguins live in the Arctic.

The North and South Poles have their own beauty. They are symbols of the strength, beauty, and danger of nature.

Name _____

☞ Read the article and highlight facts to use in the Venn diagram.

1. Highlight with yellow the facts that are the same for both the South and North Poles.
2. Highlight with blue the facts that are true only for the North Pole.
3. Highlight with red the facts that are true only for the South Pole.

Write at least four facts about each pole in the Venn diagram. Write at least four things they have in common where the circles intersect.

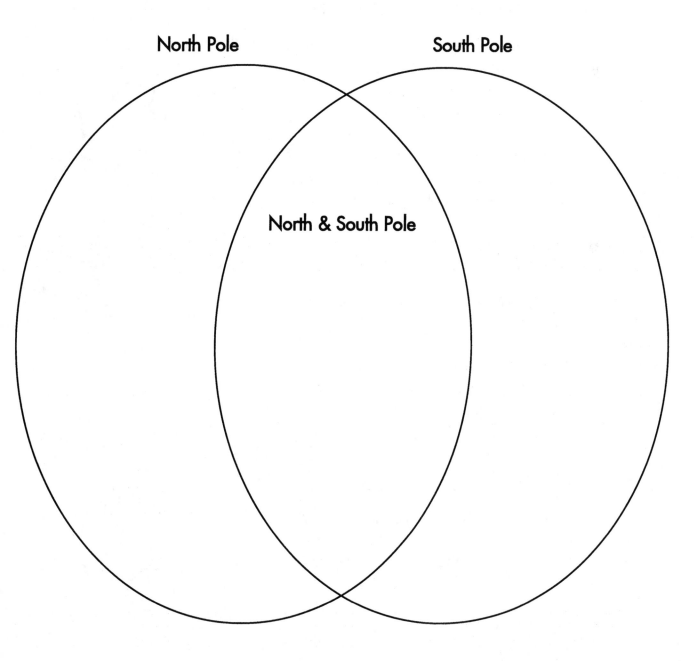

North Pole   South Pole

North & South Pole

What Does It Mean?

☞ Read each paragraph. Look at the underlined figure of speech. Put an X in front of the best meaning for the saying.

1. Joe and Gabby needed information for their report on theropods. It was hard to find resources on this dinosaur. They decided not to get another topic. They would <u>leave no stone unturned</u> while looking for information.

_____ They would look for information everywhere.

_____ They planned to turn over a lot of stones on the playground.

_____ They would look under many things.

2. Hank was out of ideas. He decided <u>two heads are better than one</u>. He asked his friend Obed to help him with his problem-solving assignment.

_____ Looking at two heads is better than looking at one.

_____ Two people thinking together come up with better ideas than one person can by himself.

_____ Two of anything is better than one.

3. The teacher walked down the hallway to get a new pack of pencils. While he was gone, his students ran around the room, yelled, and threw paper wads. He walked back in and said, "<u>When the cat's away, the mice will play</u>."

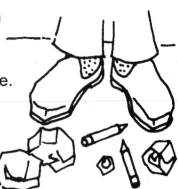

_____ Mice play with the cat's toys when the cat is gone.

_____ People don't behave as well when the person in charge is gone.

_____ Cats like to eat mice.

4. Sally got her hamburger and fries. Then she saw her friend Pat had a chicken sandwich with a chocolate shake. Sally wished she had gotten what Pat had. She asked Pat if she wanted to trade. "No," said Pat. "<u>You know the grass is always greener on the other side of the fence.</u>"

____ What someone else has always looks better.

____ If you water your grass as much as your neighbor does, you will have green grass too.

____ The way the light shines on the other side of a fence makes the grass look greener.

5. Bill hit a baseball through the window. When his dad asked him how it happened, he lied and said his sister had done it. His dad had seen him do it. Now he was <u>out of the frying pan and into the fire.</u>

____ The baseball had fallen into a frying pan and then bounced into the fireplace.

____ Frying pans usually sit on top of fire so you have to be careful not to spill things.

____ Bill was in more trouble now than he had been to start with.

6. Rebecca didn't finish her math homework last night. She played on the computer instead. She asked her mother to tell her teacher that she had been sick. Her mother told her that she would have to <u>face the music herself.</u>

____ When you play the piano, you must look at the music sheets.

____ Her teacher would ask her a musical question.

____ She must be honest with her teacher and accept the consequences.

Little Lamb

☞ Before reading the article, fold the page on the dotted line. Read each pair of statements and write a T in front of the statement you believe is true. After reading the article, go over your choices. Mark an X in front of the right answer. Write the sentence number where the correct answer is found in the text.

1. ____ Mary Had a Little Lamb is a Mother Goose rhyme.

     ____ Mary Had a Little Lamb is believed to be written by Sarah Josepha Hale.

Sentence(s) _____

2. ____ The poem was first published in 1830.

     ____ The poem was first published in the 1600s.

Sentence(s) _____

3. ____ Thomas Edison's first words on a telephone were, "Mary had a little lamb."

     ____ Thomas Edison's first recorded words on a phonograph recording were "Mary had a little lamb."

Sentence(s) _____

- -

1. Most people know the poem that begins, "Mary had a little lamb./Its fleece was white as snow." 2. The story about Mary and her lamb is told to small children. 3. They know what the teacher does when that cute little lamb stops the learning in the classroom. 4. She throws the lamb out! 5. What most children don't know is the story behind the poem. 6. Many people believe it is simply one of the Mother Goose nursery rhymes.

7. While it is included in many Mother Goose books, this poem did not start out as a Mother Goose rhyme. 8. It was written by Sarah Josepha Hale. 9. It was first published in 1830. 10. The title at that time was Mary's Lamb. 11. Mrs. Hale published it with music in her School Song Book in 1834. 12. The poem was published again in 1844. 13. This time it was added to a school book called The First Eclectic Reader. 14. In this book, the writer and editor did not give Mrs. Hale credit for writing the poem. 15. That is when most people came to believe it was a Mother Goose nursery rhyme.

16. The poem became part of scientific history in 1877. 17. At that time, Thomas Edison, the inventor, made the first phonograph recording. 18. The very first words that he recorded were, "Mary had a little lamb."

Which Money?

☞ Some of the first coins issued by the United States in the 1700s had different names than what we have today. Use the clues to fill in the problem-solving matrix. Then refer to the table to answer the questions below.

Clues:

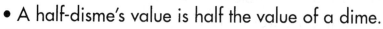

- The half-eagle is worth five dollars.
- Disme is the former name for a dime.
- A fugio cent is not worth ten dollars.
- A half-disme's value is half the value of a dime.

	$10.00	$5.00	$0.10	$0.05	$0.01
half-disme					
eagle					
fugio cent					
disme					
half-eagles					

1. A half-disme had a value of _____
   What coin do we have today that is worth the original value of a half-disme?
   _____.

2. An eagle had a value of _____ .

3. A fugio cent had a value of _____ .

   What coin do we have today that is worth the original value of a fugio cent?
   _____.

4. A disme had a value of _____ .

5. A half-eagle had a value of _____ .

Name _____

Star-Spangled Banner

☞ Before reading the article on the next page, read each pair of statements and mark an T in front of the statement you believe is true. After reading the article, go over your choices. Make an X in front of the correct answer. Write the paragraph number where the correct answer is found in the text.

1. ___ Francis Scott Key wrote the words to "The Star-Spangled Banner."
   ___ Francis Scott Key wrote the music for "The Star-Spangled Banner."
   paragraph ___

2. ___ The song was written during the Revolutionary War.
   ___ The song was written during the war of 1812.
   paragraph ___

3. ___ Francis Scott Key was a newspaper reporter.
   ___ Francis Scott Key was a lawyer.
   paragraph ___

4. ___ George Washington was president when the song was written.
   ___ James Madison was president when the song was written.
   paragraph ___

5. ___ Mr. Key was on a British warship when he wrote the song.
   ___ Mr. Key was in an American fort when he wrote the song.
   paragraph ___

6. ___ The British were attacking Baltimore.
   ___ The British were attacking Washington, D.C.
   paragraph ___

7. ___ The flag Mr. Key was watching was made by Betsy Ross.
   ___ The flag Mr. Key was watching was made by Mary Pickersgill and her daughter Caroline.
   paragraph ___

8. ___ The song's original name was "The Defense of Fort McHenry."
   ___ The song's original name was "Oh, How I Love the Flag."
   paragraph ___

9. ___ The song became the national anthem in 1834.
   ___ The song became the national anthem in 1931.
   paragraph ___

Name _____

1. "The Star Spangled Banner" was written by Francis Scott Key in 1814. The War of 1812 was in its third year.

2. Dr. Beanes, a friend of Francis Scott Key, was a prisoner on a British ship. Friends contacted Mr. Key, a Washington, D.C. lawyer, about the matter. He had to get permission from the president to speak with the British general. Mr. Key went to President Madison and was allowed to visit the British fleet under a flag of truce.

3. Francis traveled from Washington, D.C., to Baltimore. He went aboard a British ship to speak with the general. After talking with Mr. Key, General Ross agreed to let Dr. Beanes go. However, the release had to wait until after the British attacked Baltimore.

4. Francis Scott Key and Dr. Beanes were moved to another British ship, the Surprise. They traveled up Chesapeake Bay to Fort McHenry. Mr. Key could see the new American flag flying over the fort. The flag was made by Mary Pickersgill and her daughter, Caroline. It

was 42 x 30 feet (12.8 x 9.1 meters) and had fifteen stars and fifteen stripes.

5. The battle was very noisy and very smoky. It was difficult to see the fort from the ship. It seemed that the British would win the battle and the fort would surrender. As long as the American flag was flying, Mr. Key knew that there was hope. As the sun went down, those on the ship could just make out the American flag. It stormed all night long. In the morning, the storm and the battle were both over. The American flag was still flying.

6. Francis Scott Key began to write the first words, "O say can you see," on the back of an old letter he had in his pocket. He wrote a bit more, but had to put it away because the British fleet was leaving. He and Mr. Beanes went ashore. Later that night, Francis finished the poem.

7. The next day, he showed the poem to his brother-in-law who told him to publish it. His brother-in-law added the title "The Defense of Fort McHenry." Soon, however, everyone was calling it "The Star-Spangled Banner."

8. "The Star-Spangled Banner" become the U.S. national anthem in 1931. Congress made a decree to give the song its National-anthem status 117 years after its words were composed.

Flu

☞ Before reading the article on page 115, read each pair of statements and mark a T in front of the statement you believe is correct. After reading the article, go over your choices. Make an X in front of the right answer. Write the paragraph number where the correct answer is found.

1. ___   Flu and influenza are two different illnesses.
   ___   Flu and influenza are the same.
   paragraph ____

2. ___   Flu is caused by a virus.
   ___   Flu is caused by bacteria.
   paragraph ____

3. ___   Flu is a name for one illness.
   ___   Flu is the name for many related illnesses.
   paragraph ____

4. ___   One type of flu is called symptoms.
   ___   A symptom is something that indicates you have the flu.
   paragraph ____

5. ___   The main symptoms of flu are sore throat and high fever.
   ___   The main symptoms of flu are high fever, aches, cough and runny nose.
   paragraph ____

6. ___   If your nose is runny, you should not take medicine.
   ___   A runny nose is a flu symptom you can treat with medicine.
   paragraph ____

7. ___   An antibiotic will help cure the flu.
   ___   An antibiotic will not help cure the flu.
   paragraph ____

8. ___   If you have the flu, you should rest and treat the symptoms.
   ___   You should always see your doctor if you have the flu.
   paragraph ____

9. ___   Flu changes each year, so getting a flu shot every year is good.
   ___   Once you get a flu shot, you will not get the flu.
   paragraph ____

Name _____

1. You feel awful. Your head hurts. Your nose is stuffy. You have a fever. You feel achy all over. All you want to do is get a hug and go back to bed. Mom doesn't even question if you are really sick because you look sick. You know school isn't in the plans for today.

2. What is happening to you? You probably have the flu. Flu is short for influenza. Influenza is caused by a virus. Unfortunately, no antibiotics will help when you have the flu since they don't work on viruses. Your mother may call the doctor, but you probably won't have to go into the doctor's office. If, however, you have a very sore throat, the doctor may want to check your throat to make sure it isn't strep. Strep should be treated with antibiotics. Also, if the symptoms continue for several days or complications occur, you will need to see the doctor. Most doctors' offices will let you know when you should be seen by the doctor.

3. Usually, people are told to treat the symptoms. The symptoms are the things happening to your body that show you have the flu. You will probably be given some medicine to bring your fever down, or possibly for the headache or muscle aches. If you have a cough or runny nose, it may mean another medicine. Some types of influenza also cause nausea and vomiting. If that happens, you will probably drink lots of

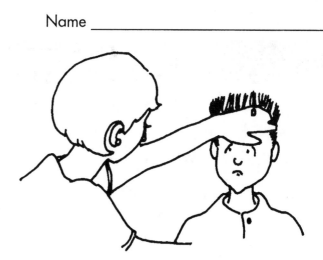

water and eat only crackers until the throwing-up stops.

4. For several days, all you will want to do is lie around and sleep. Even watching TV or reading a book will make you feel worse. Once the fever breaks, or goes down, you may feel up to doing a few things.

5. Each year, in the fall, doctors have a flu shot available for people who want it. The shot helps your body make antibodies for the several kinds of flu. That means that the body will be able to protect itself against those types of flu if it comes in contact with them. However, flu viruses change quickly, and the shot can only protect against the certain flu viruses it is made for. If the flu viruses change enough, the shot will not work.

6. If you have the flu, get ready with your most comfortable blanket and favorite pillow. Keep plenty of clear fluids at hand so you do not become dehydrated. Then, curl up with a good book or some soft music and be ready for some dream time.

Name _____

Horseshoe Crab

☞ Before reading the article on page 117, read each pair of statements and draw a T in front of the statement you believe is correct. After reading the article, go over your choices. Draw an X in front of the right answer. Write the paragraph number where the correct answer is found.

1. ___ A carapace is a shell.
   ___ A carapace is a sudden drop off.
   paragraph ___

2. ___ Horseshoes are a type of crab.
   ___ Horseshoes are related to spiders.
   paragraph ___

3. ___ A telson is a body part that looks like a tail.
   ___ A telson is a body part used to communicate.
   paragraph ___

4. ___ The horseshoe crab's tail is used as a weapon.
   ___ The horseshoe crab's tail is used to flip itself over.
   paragraph ___

5. ___ The horseshoe crab's blood is red.
   ___ The horseshoe crab's blood is blue.
   paragraph ___

6. ___ Scientists use horseshoe crab blood to stop poisons.
   ___ Scientists use horseshoe crab blood to make poisons.
   paragraph ___

7. ___ Scientists use horseshoe crab's eyes for research.
   ___ Their eyes are used to make a delicious dessert.
   paragraph ___

8. ___ Limulus polyphemus is the scientific name for a horseshoe crab.
   ___ Limulus polyphemus is the name of a scientist who studies crabs.
   paragraph ___

9. ___ Horseshoe crabs are scavengers who eat ocean garbage.
   ___ Horseshoe crabs eat clams, worms, and invertebrates.
   paragraph ___

1. The horseshoe crab lives in oceans around the world. It is often called a living fossil. The scientific name of this animal is Limulus polyphemus. Limulus polyphemus has been on earth for about 20 million years, but fossils of its close relatives have been found that are around 500 million years old.

2. The horseshoe crab is not really a crab. It is related to spiders, scorpions and ticks. This creature has a domed carapace, or shell, that is shaped a bit like a horseshoe. It has five pairs of legs underneath which end in claws. The mouth is found at the base of these legs. The horseshoe crab eats clams, worms, and invertebrates. It breathes with six pair of special gills called bill books.

3. The tail of the horseshoe crab is called a telson. It is attached to the shell with a hinge joint. This joint works like our elbow joints. The telson helps the horseshoe crab flip back over after a wave has tipped it upside down.

4. Most horseshoe crabs spend their lives within 4 miles of where they hatch. These creatures begin as 2- or 3-millimeter eggs. They can grow to be 60 centimeters, or 24 inches long. As the horseshoe crab grows, it molts, or sheds, its too-small shell.

5. The blood of a horseshoe crab is not red like ours. It has a molecule that turns it a bluish color when exposed to the air. This molecule carries the oxygen through its body.

6. Scientist use horseshoe crabs in research. Horseshoe crabs have two sets of eyes. One set of eyes, called compound eyes, is made up of many tiny eyes. The other set is simple, like human eyes. Scientists study these eyes to learn how human eyes work.

7. The horseshoe crab is used for other research. Scientists have found that a fluid in the horseshoe crab can be used to make human blood coagulate, or thicken. Scientists are careful not to harm the horseshoe crabs when they remove the fluid and return them to their homes. Then scientists use a chemical found in the fluid to stop the effect of some poisons in human blood.

8. Odd and unique, this creature has lived on this earth for a long time. It is an interesting animal that has proven helpful to scientists and worth looking at to those who run across them at the beach.

Name _____

Famous African-Americans

☞ Read the clues about these highly distinguished African-Americans. Use the clues to figure out the birth date of each famous American below.

- A 44-year old woman was elected to the US Congress in 1968.
- Matthew Henson was born before the 1900s.
- The astronaut was born 211 years after Benjamin Banneker.
- Thurgood Marshall turned eleven the year Jackie Robinson was born.

	1731	1866	1908	1919	1924	1942
Jackie Robinson first African-American to play major league baseball						
Matthew Henson one of the first explorers of the North Pole						
Benjamin Banneker helped design Washington, DC; determined location of streets and buildings						
Guy Bluford first African-American astronaut to go into space						
Shirley Chisholm first elected African-American Congresswoman						
Thurgood Marshall first African-American Supreme Court justice						

What year were they born?

Jackie Robinson _____   Matthew Henson _____   Guy Bluford _____

Benjamin Banneker _____   Shirley Chisholm _____   Thurgood Marshall _____

What two men were born before 1900? _____

What was the major accomplishment of the man born in 1919?

Answer Key

When and Where (setting) 4
1. When: November
   Where: football field
2. When: evening
   Where: outside under the stars
3. When: afternoon in July, 1776
   Where: in the common area in Boston
4. When: in the future
   Where: in a spaceship

Now or Later (setting) 5
1. past
   key word(s) 1492
2. present
   key word(s) is working (present tense)
3. present
   key word(s) is hot (present tense)
4. future
   key word(s) trip to Jupiter
5. past
   key word(s) Brachiosaurus
6. future
   key word(s) grandmother in third grade back
   around 2000

What's the Problem?
(identifying characters and problems) 6
1. Characters: Nick and Tanner
   Problem: Nick fell while skating and hurt his
   hands.
2. Character: Bonnie Butterfly:
   Problem: Bonnie is still learning to land and is
   afraid of landing.
3. Characters: Dan and Joe (Mrs. Willis)
   Problem: Dan has been daydreaming rather than
   working.
4. Characters: Pitter and Patter
   Problem: Pitter is separating from her friend.

The Trip (story elements) 7
When: on a hot spring day
Where: on a deserted road in the desert
Characters: Abby and her family
Problem: Their car broke down at the beginning of
   Abby's spring vacation.
Predictions will vary, but should fit the story.

Decision (story elements) 8
When: on a spring morning
Where: on the way to school
Characters: Heath (and Shane)
Problem: Heath must decide if he should skip school

with his best friend.
Predictions will vary, but should fit the story.

Water's Edge (story elements) 9
When: evening
Where: on a beach
Characters: Gabe and Hannah
Problem: Gabe wants to know more about horseshoe
   crabs.
Gabe will probably ask to meet Hannah's sister and
   learn more about horseshoe crabs.

Power's Out (problem and solution) 10
Television out: Use a battery-powered radio to get
   weather information.
Well not working: Fill empty milk jugs with fresh
   water before the storm.
Furnace won't start: Find extra blankets or purchase a
   generator to run the furnace.
Stove doesn't work: Eat fruit, bread, and peanut
   butter.
Dark in the house: Use a flashlight, lantern, or
   candles to light the area.

Highlighting Information
(reading for details) 11
1. light-colored crayon, pencil, or marker
2. read, scan, and highlight
3. word or phrase
4. mark over the words lightly
   underline the words
5. copied pages, testing materials, newspapers, or
   your own books

Which Resource? (reading for details) 12
1. index
2. atlas
3. glossary
4. dictionary
5. thesaurus
6. encyclopedia or atlas
7. encyclopedia
8. thesaurus
9. index

Rainsticks (reading for details) 13
1. the skeleton of a cactus
2. a type of cactus
3. Tiny stones pour across the thorns.
4. a cactus skeleton, thorns, and stones
5. calm, quiet, and soothing; Synonyms will vary.

Wolf Talk (reading for details) 14–15
1. It is telling another wolf it is the boss.
2. It wants to play.
3. It is telling another wolf it is the boss.
4. It doesn't want any trouble.
5. It doesn't want any trouble.
6. It wants to play.
7. Answers will vary.

Red Tide (reading for details) 16–17
1. Scientists hope to learn why red tide happens so they can warn people when the water is not safe.
2. saltwater
3. nutrients and sunlight
4. irritatied eyes, nose, and throats; lips and tongues tingle; can make people sick; hard to breathe
5. multiply means increase
6. dinoflagellate
7. It is warm; People like to swim or play in the sun; There are interesting plants and animals.
8. people who like to look for shells
9. stay away from the beach

A Beautiful Butterfly (reading for details) 18–19
Life cycle sketch should include adult, egg, caterpillar, and chrysalis.
1. monarch butterfly
2. about the monarch life cycle
3. adult, egg, caterpillar, and chrysalis
4. yellow, black, and white
5. 16 legs
6. ten days
7. milkweed plants
8. J shape
9. one week
10. 15 minutes
11. orange, black, and white
12. six legs
13. migrate south
14. fly back north to lay eggs

Math Homework (reading for details) 20
1. ones column
2. number 9; Subtract the ones.
3. number 5; Pretend you are picking up a cup of ten. Cross out the top tens digit.
4. no   no   yes   no

Pizza Recipe (reading for details) 21
1. choose three from pepperoni, mushrooms, pineapple, sausage, or olives
2. yes; the words "your favorite toppings," plus etc. imply that others are okay.

3. no, it calls for soft tortillas
4. 350°; for 10 minutes
5. tomato sauce
6. cheese goes on before the toppings
7. Answers will vary; The answer comes from the student's head.

Note Home (reading for details) 22–23
1. setting, characters, problem, and solution
2. Wednesday
3. send a note by Friday
4. study sheet and questions for the social studies test
5. through field tests
6. three-digit numbers
7. Thursday
8. $1.50 per student
9. Tuesday
10. Reminders will vary. Suggestions:
Monday: Remember an old shirt for art.
Tuesday: Remember library book
Wednesday: Lunch money is due.
Thursday: Social studies test today
Friday: Remember gym shoes.

Book Offer (reading for details) 24–25
1. books
2. seven books
3. six additional books
4. one year
5. 99¢ for each book
6. F
   T
   F
   T
7. not given
8. not given
9. not given
10. Explanations will vary, but students should indicate that the offer is misleading.

Cancel It (reading for details) 26
1. She would like to purchase a cassette. She is canceling her membership.
2. no, a free cassette tape
3. 16 Tan Street
   Troy, MI 49000
4. her membership number
5. business letter; It is addressed to "To Whom It May Concern."

Understanding Food Labels
(reading for details) 27
1. Cracker A is larger. Five crackers have a mass of 30

grams, while five of cracker B have only 15 grams.
2. Cracker B has the highest number of calories. Thirty grams has 160 calories.
3. Cracker A must be larger because a smaller number of crackers adds up to 30 grams.
4. Cracker A has only 70 calories for 30 g.

Flags (following directions) 28–29
Ghana   Australia
Africa   Australia
It borders the   Kangaroos live there.
Atlantic Ocean.

China   Guatemala
Asia   Central America
Mount Everest   Has 27 volcanoes.
is located there.

Netherlands   Brazil
Europe   South America
It is below sea   Amazon River basin is
level.   located there.

Marshmallows (story details) 30
Pictures will vary.

Starting Out Right (topic sentences) 31
1. Snow is lots of fun.
2. Ian is a good reader.
3. Don't put your tongue on ice-cold metal.
4. School is important.

What's the Point? (topic sentences) 32
1. Breakfast is good for you for many reasons. (Topic sentences will vary.)
   pronoun: it
   topic: breakfast
   point of paragraph: breakfast is good for you.
2. The computer makes writing easier. (Topic sentences will vary.)
   pronoun: it
   topic: computer
   point of paragraph: The computer makes writing easier.
3. Deer are herbivores. (Topic sentences will vary.)
   pronoun: they
   topic: deer
   point of paragraph: What deer eat.

Sharp Pencils & Sharp Minds
(main idea and supporting details) 33
Topic: sharp pencils
Main idea: It is important to know when to sharpen

your pencil so that learning is not interrupted
Supporting details: sharpen before or after school; sharpen when others are not listening to directions; sharpening pencils can be distracting; keep an extra sharp pencil in your desk.
Topic: getting enough sleep
Main idea: Getting enough sleep is important.
Supporting details: rest improves attitude; keeps thinking sharp; helps people get along with others; gives energy.

Wolves (identifying supporting details) 34
Details may vary.
Topic sentence: After the settlement of the Europeans in the US, the wolf population quickly became endangered.
First main detail and minor supporting details: Wolves were gone from most of the west; wolves were killed and they moved away from people.
Second main detail and minor supporting details: Some wolves were brought back to parks and wild regions; some wolves moved from Canada and scientists are watching their progress.

Long Necks
(identifying supporting details) 35
Details may vary.
Topic sentence: Paleontologists have found many long-necked dinosaurs that lived in the Jurassic period.
First main detail and minor supporting details: One dinosaur is the Brachiosaurus; it was 70 feet long and its front legs were longer than its hind legs.
Second main detail and minor supporting details: Another dinosaur is the Apatosaurus; it was 70 feet long and its front legs were shorter than its hind legs.
Third main detail and minor supporting details: Another dinosaur is Diplodocus; it was 88 feet long and it used its tail as a weapon.

Great Lakes
(identifying supporting details) 36
Details may vary.
Topic sentence: Many states border the five Great Lakes in the United States.
First main detail and minor supporting details: One state is Michigan; it touches four lakes and a bridge joins two lakes.
Second main detail and minor supporting details: Another state is Wisconsin; it touches two lakes and is a popular site for boat launching and fishing.

Third main detail and minor supporting details:
Another state is Illinois; it contains the city of
Chicago and is visited by boaters and swimmers.

Messy Desk (summary) 37
1. He decides what has to go into his desk.
2. He finds a place for everything.
3. He cleans his desk every Tuesday.
4. Whenever he takes something out, he puts it back
in its place.
Topic sentence: Keeping your desk clean takes planning and time.

Deep in the Earth (main idea) 38–39
Topic: rocks
Main idea: Rocks are formed three ways.
Topic sentence: There are three kinds of rocks.
Sub-topics: igneous rocks; sedimentary rock; and
metamorphic rocks
Supporting details: Igneous rocks are formed deep
inside the earth's core; when lava cools, it forms
igneous rocks. Sedimentary rock is made up of
loose materials in water that dissolve and get
cemented together. Metamorphic rocks are formed
by a major change; it may even change its mineral
makeup.

Solids, Liquids, and Gases
(main idea) 40
Topic: matter
Main idea: matter has three states.
Chart:
Solids—yes—yes—no—rocks, cork, and cookies
Liquids—yes—yes—yes—water, milk, and pop
Gases—yes—yes—yes—oxygen, hydrogen, and
carbon dioxide

A Night in Texas (reading for details) 41
1. in Austin, Texas
2. bats
3. Bats are gentle. They sleep during the day and eat
bugs. (Answers may vary.)
4. clouds to bats; sun to electric blanket; her weight
to the weight of the bugs
5. (Answers may vary.) Bats are gentle; they do not
attack people. Bats eat bugs.

Walk by Water (inferencing) 42
1. dawn; "The last star fades as the sun peeks over
the horizon."
2. Florida; It is the only state of the three that has
access to an ocean.
3. a week

4. excited
5. curious, happy

Kali and Koko (inferencing) 43
1. dogs; "The only response was far-off barking.
They've cornered something, she thought."
2. She smelled the skunk that the dogs encountered.
She didn't want the dogs to jump on her with that
scent all over them.
3. They were sprayed by a skunk. The details that
helped: the yelps and silence followed by the
stench. Jenny told the dogs they would need to stay
outside for a couple days.

It's That Time (inferencing) 44
1. autumn
2. evening
3. supper
4. Wisconsin; the other states do not have the red
and brown fall leaves and the southbound geese in
the fall.
5. peaceful
6. Ned is Sally's dog.
7. Sketch should show a shaggy dog.

Figure It Out (idioms) .45
1. Gina is a good gardener.
2. It was raining really hard.
3. The puppy made Pia and Tio very tired.
4. Rita just had to smile.
5. Kee will change what he is doing and make it
better.

Chocolate Bars (inferencing) 46–47
Sequence
5 Milton Hershey sold Hershey bars for 5¢ each.
1 People made a bitter drink from chocolate.
6 You can enjoy a chocolate candy bar.
4 Hershey mass produced milk chocolate.
3 Peter and Nestlé produce milk chocolate.
2 A Dutch chemist makes cocoa powder.

1. chocolate
2. chocolate was not sweetened and not readily available.
3. expensive; It took a long time to make.
4. make it in large amounts in a factory
5. He found a way to mass produce milk chocolate
and sold it inexpensively.
6. No, but bitter chocolate was available. They used
chocolate in a drink with spices.
7. Answers will vary as they come from the students'
heads.

Ralph (character analysis) 48
1. Ralph is a dog.
2. No; he is dirty and hungry.
3. Yes; he has a collar.
4. She does not like Ralph; she has swatted him with a broom and sprayed him with a hose before.
5. Drawings will vary, but should show a dirty dog with very long hair.

What Happens Next? (predicting) 49
1. The marbles will roll off the table and onto the floor.
2. Zoe will stay in and finish her math.
3. Jeryl's mom will help her wash her knee.
4. Evan will ask the librarian if any insect books have been returned.

Venus Flytrap (predicting) 50
1. Venus flytrap
2. Her plant didn't look well and she wanted to read about how to care for the plant.
3. The plant is carnivorous.
4. meat-eating
5. Answers will vary. Kayla will go home and feed her new plant meat.

Cranberries (sequencing) 51
1. Massachusetts and Wisconsin
2. dying rugs and blankets
3. Sequence:
   4
   6
   1
   2
   7
   3
   5

Honey (sequencing) 52
1. nursemaids, cleaners, guards, or nectar collectors
2. one teaspoon
3. A bee follows directions given by another bee in the form of a dance.
4. Sequence:
   1
   3
   5
   4
   2

Coins (vocabulary) 53
1. a factory where coins are made
2. to make by stamping
3. a mold

4. the same every time
5. having the same size and value

Water Cycle (sequencing) 54–55

Patter	Pitter
6	2
2	4
1	6
4	5
X (cross out)	X (cross out)
3	1
5	3

Venn diagram:
Patter: was digested by a dog
Pitter: soaked into the ground; traveled underground and in a lake
Both: became heated and went up into the sky; were part of a cloud

Northern Lights (reading for details) 56
1. aurora borealis
2. ten to twenty minutes
3. on the sun
4. atmosphere
5. like water from a hose that someone swings in a circle over his head
6. a storm of particles hitting the atmosphere
7. The plasma particles stop striking.

Which Meaning? (context clues) 57
1. B
2. C
3. A
4. C
5. A
6. B
7. C
8. A
9. B

A Switch Is a Switch (context clues) 58
1. B
2. C
3. A
4. C
5. C
6. Words and sentences will vary.

Think About It (fact or opinion) 59
1. opinion; deserved
2. fact
3. fact
4. opinion; beautiful

5. fact
6. opinion; easy
7. fact
8. fact
9. fact
10. opinion; great
11. fact
12. fact
13. fact
14. opinion; beautiful and hard
15. opinion; interesting
16. opinion; easy

Animals On Parade
(fact or opinion) 60
1. fact
2. opinion; interesting
3. fact
4. fact
5. opinion; should not
6. fact
7. opinion; creepy
8. opinion; sneaky
9. opinion; fun
10. opinion; should
11. opinion; beautiful
12. fact
13. opinion; disgusting
14. fact
15. fact
16. fact

Sports Report (fact or opinion) 61
Opinion words in article include pathetic, terrible,
    hard, sad, beautiful, exciting, perfect, should,
    hope, outstanding, difficult, dependable, awe-
    some, fabulous, impressive, and more.
Dogs and Wild Ones: The Dogs lost. The Dogs had
    12 points at the end of the first quarter. The Dogs
    have won in the past.
Mudpies and Quicksanders: The score was close.
    The Quicksanders won. The score at the end was
    77–78.
Kilometers and Miles: The Kilometers won. The final
    score was 86–68. Decka scored 43 points. Van
    Inch and Mc Yard each scored 22 points.

Packing (compare and contrast) 62
1. Items packed correctly (students highlight all, then
    choose one): sweatshirts, jeans, sunglasses, beach
    shoes
2. (choose 2) underwear, spring jacket, toothbrush,
    and pajamas
3. (choose 2) shorts, socks, beach towels, and tennis

shoes
4. (choose 1) turtleneck, short-sleeved shirt, under-
    wear, pajamas, spring jacket, and toothbrush
5. one more turtleneck
6. five more pairs of underwear
7. Answers will vary, but students should indicate
    that planning will prevent being without something
    important when away from home.

Two Events (compare and contrast) 63
1. Both
   Carnival
   Both
   Carnival
2. Pond Life; boots or waders; bring to wade in the
    pond.
3. Pond Life
4. outdoor activities
5. F
   T
   T
   F

Florida and Michigan (compare and contrast) 64
Florida: bordered by salt water; water creatures
    include sharks, jellyfish, and dolphins; find sea
    shells; warm all year; crops include oranges and
    coconuts
Michigan: bordered by fresh water, fish include
    salmon and trout; has sandy beaches; hot in sum-
    mer; cold in winter; fruits include blueberries,
    apples, cherries, and peaches.
Both: pennisula states (surrounded by water) and
    attract tourists

How Did It Happen? (cause and effect) 65
1. Bluebirds made a nest.
2. It was ruined.
3. Jackie skipped breakfast.
4. She smiled.
5. He will play at recess.
6. Mom went to see the baby. (This is the missing
    effect and the missing cause.)

Sand Dune (cause and effect) 66
1. He had just climbed a sand dune.
2. William was high up and the cars looked small.
3. When he ran down the hill, the sand filled his
    shoes.
4. He had so much fun running down the hill, he
    wanted her to have fun, too.

Coin Collecting (cause and effect) 67
Cause: Most Americans were too busy building a
country out of a wilderness to think about coins.
Cause: In 1857, the United States stopped making
the large-sized coin.
Cause: Coin collecting became very popular.

What a Disaster! (cause and effect) 68–69
1. Nell forgot to set her alarm last night so she is late
for class.
2. Answers will vary. She should call and tell the
school she is late and walk in the hall.
3. Answers will vary. Possible responses: Chris will
not get credit for the work he did. Nell will help
him recreate it. He will explain his project to the
class.
Answers for missing parts of the chart:
Cause: Nell didn't set the alarm.
Cause: Nell is late.
Effect: Chris's project falls to the floor.
Effect: Chris bends down to pick up his things.
Cause: Chris slips on the liquid.
Cause: Chris grabs Nell's leg.
Effect: The teacher comes out into the hallway.
Cause: Nell has twisted her ankle.

The Storm (cause and effect) 70–71
Pictures will vary.
Answers for missing parts of the chart:
Effect: The electricity went out.
Cause: The electricity went out.
Effect: Kitty jumped to the counter.
Cause: The marbles fell and made a big noise.
Effect: They made a loud noise and knocked over the
flour.
Cause: The flashlight batteries died and he could not
see.
Effect: He upset the marble jar and they scattered all
over the floor.
Cause: The cat landed on the cookie sheet.
Cause: The marbles were all over the floor.
Effect: Everything was covered with white.
Cause: The events in the kitchen made a loud noise.

Commercials (author's purpose) 72–73
1. The author wishes to persuade you to think about
what commercials are selling.
2. They are entertaining, thought-provoking, and can
trigger your emotions.
3. Commercials may convince you that you need
something that you do not need.
4. A feeling inside that you need something
5. The button on the television that turns it off.

6. Answers will vary.
7. Answers will vary.

Tall Tales (fact and fantasy) 74
1. X; purple dog flying
2. could be true
3. could be true
4. X; picked a quarter from the vine
5. X; row stretches from the South Pole to the North
Pole.
6. could be true
7. X; warned the alien to get back inside (his backpack)
8. X; score was one million to zero

Bees (main idea) 75
1. The author wishes to teach about bees.
2. Bees are very important to us.
They pollinate plants.
If plants are not pollinated, seeds are not made.
3. Bees are in trouble.
Mites kill baby bees.
Chemicals kill bees.

Visiting Grandparents (author's viewpoint) 76
1. Shopping; He didn't have much to say about it.
2. Watching the fish at the pond; He wrote a lot
about it and wrote with excitement.
3. Visiting the caves; He wrote a lot, used humor, and
bought a postcard to remember the experience.

Reading Goals (author's viewpoint) 77
1. She is pleased that she reached her goal. "I really
like reading now."
2. Her goal was to read at a 3.5 level, but she is
reading at a higher level (3.75).
3. I read every day. I made sure what I read made
sense. I paid attention in reading class.

Puzzles (author's viewpoint) 78
1. The author liked cleaning up; things looked nice
when they were done cleaning.
2. The author thought it was right. The author argued
that Tanner should have cleaned it up or told
someone he would clean it up later.
3. Wrong; Tanner shoved the author.

Pencils (reading a chart) 79
1. T
2. F
3. F
4. F
5. T
6. F

7. T
8. F
9. F
Recommendations will vary, but should be supported
   with data from the chart.

Letter to Grandma (author's viewpoint) 80–81
1. good: likes sledding and building snowmen
   negative: His mom was in an accident and it is
   very cold.
2. She picked up take-out food.
   "I hope she will pick up take-out food more
   often."
3. good: likes fishing and picking up shells on the
   beach
   negative: The weather is very hot and he could get
   sunburned.

The Summer House (story details) 82–83
1. The tall grass:
   Parents think of mowing and weeding.
   Ernie thinks of finding bugs.
2. The doors and windows:
   Parents think of peeling paint and darkness.
   Ernie thinks of climbing out the window.
   The overgrown bushes and screened porch:
   Parents think of cutting back bushes and bugs get-
   ting into the porch.
   Ernie thinks of making a fort on the porch.

Vertebrates (reading a chart) 84
1. cold-blooded
2. mammals
3. fish
4. feathers
5. Choose two: have skin and hair; offspring born
   live, drink mother's milk; warm-blooded; and
   breathe with lungs.
6. Choose one: born from an egg; do not drink mother's milk; and cold-blooded.

Beverages (reading a chart) 85
1. seven
2. T
   F
   T
   F
   T

Home Runs (reading a chart) 86
1. Babe Ruth; in the text
2. Roger Maris; in the text
3. Mark McGwire; both

4. Sammy Sosa; in the chart
5. September; both
6. Same month; September; both

Insect Report (interpreting a graph) 87
1. No, more students like insects after the report.
   in the graphs
2. Insects are important for pollinating plants
   in the text
3. Answers will vary. Examples: Fewer people disliked
   insects after they heard the report. After the report,
   more people liked insects than disliked them.
4. Details to highlight include "products we use that
   depend on insect pollination;" "we have lost about
   one-fourth of the insect pollinators."

Bike Helmets (interpreting a graph) 88
1. 15
2. 26
3. 24
4. no; in the graph
5. yes
6. Choose any of the six on the graph.**
7. Opinions will vary.

Baseball (interpreting a graph) 89
1. Spuds
2. 13 games
3. 3 more wins
4. third place
5. 12 wins
6. Gizmos and Kazoos
7. seven wins to catch up

New Baby (reading a table of contents) 90
1. page 83
2. page 60
3. "If I Were an Only Child"
4. "Two A.M. Crying"
5. "You Can Have Her; She's Free"
6. "The New Baby"
7. 15 pages
8. 8 chapters
9. "A Trip to the Zoo"
   begins on page 29; ends on page 39
10. "Ga Ba Da Wa—Wov Oo"
    begins on page 72; ends on page 82; 10 pages
11. Titles will vary. There Is a New Baby in My
    House

Science Book (reading a table of contents) 91
1. Sound
2. how a solid chanes to a liquid; This is a physical

change, not just the difference in states of matter.
3. pages 70–85
4. how a seed grows into a seedling, then a plant which produces a seed; This chapter is about the plant cycle.
5. Unit 3, chapter 3; This is about weathering.

A Year in My Life
(reading a table of contents) 92–93
1. C
2. D
3. C
4. B
5. B
6. B
7. C

Nursery Rhyme Ads (critical thinking) 94

Little Jack Horner   Peter Piper
Old Woman in Shoe   Mary Had a Little Lamb
Jack and Jill   Sixpence
Old Mother Hubbard
Humpty Dumpty   Wee Willie Winkie

Fairy Tale Headlines (critical thinking) 95

Three Little Pigs 12 Dancing   Jack and the
                   Princesses   Beanstalk
Snow White   Sleeping Beauty Beauty and the
                                   Beast

Baby Book (interpreting a time line) 96
1. six months
2. in front, bottom right
   eight and a half months
3. rolled over from tummy to back
4. squeals at four months; sits at six
5. nine months; likes carrots, but doesn't like plums

Family Tree (reading a diagram) 97
1. (Dan, Jess, Debbie, and Jack) four children
2. Abe
   Hal and Kitty
   Bob and Ann
   John and Sue
3. yes—Jack; no parents; no children
4. sisters
5. Cal and Kate
6. Answers will vary. Examples: Cal and Sam; Cory and Jen; Tom and Dan; Quin and Nan

U.S. Paper Money (reading for details) 98–99
1775: paper money first issued
1785: official money system based on dollar
1860: paper money printed with green ink, like today

1865: Secret Service established to control fakes
1929: bills were all made the same size
1990: bills starting to change design to prevent faking
1999: only the 1-, 2-, 5-, 10-, 20-, 50-, and 100-dollar bills were still produced
1. money
2. 1865; established to control counterfeiting
3. give out
4. the green ink printed on the back of the bills
5. Washington, Lincoln, and Jefferson
6. 1929
7. to prevent counterfeiting

Dolphins & Porpoises (Venn diagram) 100–101
1. dolphin; Dolphins are faster. Porpoises swim up to 12 miles per hour.
2. porpoise; Porpoises have round and blunt snouts.
3. Choose two: mammals, breathe air, have lungs, related to whales, and eat fish
4. Both porpoises and dolphins may have those attributes.
   Look at the snout; dolphin's is like a bird's beak and porpoise's is round and blunt.
5. fish
6. dolphin
7. porpoise

John Glenn (Venn diagram) 102–103
1. He was the first American to circle the earth.
2. He was the oldest astronaut to orbit the earth.
3. go around, or circle (the earth)
Venn diagram:
1962: 40 years old; traveled on the Friendship 7; orbited three times; one window; was alone; no computers on board
1998: 77 years old; traveled on the Discovery shuttle; orbited the earth 144 times; ten windows; six other astronauts with him; five computers
Both Flights: purpose was to observe his reaction to the space environment; was a hero.

The Moon and Its Phases
(reading for details) 104–105
1. It reflects the light from the sun.
   in the text
2. More than half the moon; in the diagram
3. 29 days; in the text
4. earth; both
5. waxing crescent; in the diagram
6. something that orbits around a planet; in the text
7. July; in the text
8. half the moon; in the text
9. full moon; in the diagram
10. eight; both

North and South Pole
(compare and contrast) 106–107
North Pole: northern hemisphere; everywhere you
  look is south; in the Arctic; below the ice is the
  Arctic Ocean; polar bears live there
South Pole: southern hemisphere; everywhere you
  look is north; below the ice is land; Antarctica is a
  continent; penguins live there
Both: very cold; desolate; covered with ice; have a
  summer and a winter; sunlight for 24 hours during
  summer; darkness for 24 hours during winter; no
  people permanently live in the region; seals live
  there

What Does It Mean? (figure of speech) 108–109
1. They would look for information everywhere.
2. Two people thinking together come up with better
   ideas than one person can by himself.
3. People don't behave as well when the person in
   charge is gone.
4. What someone else has always looks better.
5. Bill was in more trouble now than he had been to
   start with.
6. She must be honest with her teacher and accept
   the consequences.

Little Lamb (reading for information) 110
1. Mary Had a Little Lamb is believed to be written
   by Sarah Josepha Hale. (Sentence 8)
2. The poem was first published in 1830. (Sentence
   9)
3. Thomas Edison's first recorded words on a phonograph recording were "Mary had a little lamb."
   (Sentence 18)

Which Money? (logic matrix) 111
1. $0.05; nickel
2. $10.00
3. $0.01; penny
4. $0.10
5. $5.00

Star-Spangled Banner
(reading for information) 112–113
1. Francis Scott Key wrote the words to The Star-
   Spangled Banner. (paragraph 6)
2. The song was written during the war of 1812.
   (paragraph 1)
3. Francis Scott Key was a lawyer. (paragraph 2)
4. James Madison was president when the song was
   written. (paragraph 2)
5. Mr. Key was on a British warship when he wrote
   the song. (paragraph 5—accept 4 or 6 as well)

6. The British were attacking Baltimore. (paragraph 3)
7. The flag was made by Mary Pickersgill and her
   daughter Caroline. (paragraph 4)
8. The song's original name was "The Defense of Fort
   McHenry." (paragraph 7)
9. The song became the national anthem in 1931.
   (paragraph 8)

Flu (reading for information) 114–115
1. Flu and influenza are the same. (paragraph 2)
2. Flu is caused by a virus. (paragraph 2)
3. Flu is the name for many related illnesses.
   (paragraph 5)
4. A symptom is something that indicates you have
   the flu. (paragraph 3)
5. The main symptoms of flu are high fever, aches,
   cough, and runny nose. (paragraph 3)
6. A runny nose is a flu symptom you can treat with
   medicine. (paragraph 3)
7. An antibiotic will not help cure the flu. (paragraph
   2)
8. If you have the flu, you should rest and treat the
   symptoms. (paragraph 3)
9. Flu changes each year, so getting a flu shot every
   year is good. (paragraph 5)

Horseshoe Crab (reading for information) . .116–117
1. A carapace is a shell. (paragraph 2)
2. Horseshoes are related to spiders. (paragraph 2)
3. A telson is a body part that looks like a tail. (paragraph 3)
4. The horseshoe crab's tail is used to flip itself over.
   (paragraph 3)
5. The horseshoe crab's blood is blue. (paragraph 5)
6. Scientists use horseshoe crab blood to stop poisons. (paragraph 7)
7. Scientists use horseshoe crab eyes for research.
   (paragraph 6)
8. Limulus polyphemus is the scientific name for a
   horseshoe crab. (paragraph 1)
9. Horseshoe crabs eat clams, worms, and invertebrates. (paragraph 2)

Famous African-Americans (logic matrix) 118
Jackie Robinson: 1919   Matthew Henson: 1866
Guy Bluford: 1942   Benjamin Banneker: 1731
Shirley Chisholm: 1924   Thurgood Marshall: 1908
Before 1900: Henson and Banneker
First African-American to play major league baseball